C8

SOCIAL DEMOCRATIC
PARTIES IN EUROPE

SOCIAL DEMOCRATIC PARTIES IN EUROPE

Anton Pelinka

PRAEGER

PRAEGER SPECIAL STUDIES • PRAEGER SCIENTIFIC

Library of Congress Cataloging in Publication Data

Pelinka, Anton, 1941–

  Social democratic parties in Europe.

  Translation of: Sozialdemokratie in Europa.
  Bibliography: p.
  Includes index.
  1. Socialism—Europe. 2. Socialist parties
—Europe. I. Title.
HX238.5.P4413 1983   324.24072   82-18940
ISBN 0-03-062362-6

Published in 1983 by Praeger Publishers
CBS Educational and Professional Publishing
a Division of CBS Inc.
521 Fifth Avenue, New York, New York 10175 U.S.A.

Sozialdemokratie in Europa: Macht ohne Grundsätze
oder Grundsätze ohne Macht? © 1980 by Herold Druck-u.
Verlagsgesellschaft m.b.H.
English translation © 1983 by Praeger Publishers

3456789 052 987654321

Printed in the United States of America
on acid-free paper

Preface to the American Edition

The appearance of this book in revised form in the United States surely reflects the interest of a part of the U.S. public in European Social Democracy. Despite a certain analogy to the Democratic party in the United States, the Social Democratic type of party has never been able to gain a solid footing in the United States. Yet, as a dominant type of party in the North Atlantic Treaty Organization countries of Europe, it is certainly of great interest for U.S. policy and thus for U.S. political science.

First and foremost, I wish to thank Werner Feld for his kind efforts in establishing important contacts during my guest professorship at the University of New Orleans. My thanks also go to Betsy Brown, who articulated the interest of Praeger Publishers so promptly and unbureaucratically. For the translation, my thanks go to Dennis Mercer, and for the preparation of the manuscript, once again I extend thanks to Barbara Kirchebner.

Anton Pelinka
Innsbruck, March 1982

Preface to the
Austrian Edition

This book is not a party pamphlet. It does not aim to propagandize for social democracy; it by no means intends to come out against social democracy. It is an attempt at a most sober stocktaking based on the analytical tools of political science. Still, this book is not value-free, for political science and the social sciences in general can never be value-free. The values informing the following discussion are those of a democracy embodied in the political systems of Europe that Social Democracy helped to create, a democracy that has not come to the end of its development potential.

The concept of Social Democracy is here and in the following used broadly. It applies to all Socialist and Social Democratic parties that have joined together in the Socialist International; it includes parties that for particular reasons have certain objections to the concept of social democracy—the Socialists of France, Italy, Spain, and Portugal.

I wish to extend my thanks to Walter Jambor for the stimulus to write this book. My thanks also go to Franz Horner and Michél Cullin for initial clarifying discussions. Finally, special thanks go to Barbara Kirchebner for her work in preparing the manuscript.

Anton Pelinka
Innsbruck, August 1979

Contents

List of Tables

Table		Page

1

On the Concept and Origins
of Social Democracy and
Democratic Socialism

Finally, there is the vision of socialism itself. This
is not an immediate program, constrained by what
is politically possible, or even the projection of a
middle distance in which structural changes might
take place. It is the idea of an utterly new society
in which some of the fundamental limitations of human
existence have been transcended.

Michael Harrington[1]

The concept of social democracy can be understood only
in connection with the development of the theory of socialism.
An unbroken tradition of socialism, distinct from the sundry
socialist-tinged utopias around the beginning of the modern
era, first developed in the wake of the French Revolution. At
the beginning of the nineteenth century, different theorists,
influenced by the Enlightenment and the bourgeois revolution,
formulated the concept of a socialist society. These theoretical
rudiments shared a common desire to transfer the idea of the
French Revolution into the economic realm and to translate
liberty, equality, and fraternity into the relations of production.
The theories of the early socialists were ultimately developed
and integrated into a political movement through the political
force and writings of Karl Marx and as a consequence of the
revolutions of 1848 and after. The wave of industrialization
and parliamentarization spreading through Europe at that time
prepared the ground for a political movement: the worker's
movement. On this ground socialism was to become a political
practice, a party, a Social Democracy.[2]

Social democracy was at first a broad concept for the European labor movement, a movement that saw itself primarily, though not exclusively, as Marxist. Relatively uniform around the middle of the nineteenth century, social democracy was defined by three roots and the fundamental antagonisms growing out of them.

Enlightenment and rationalism created antagonism toward the prevailing understanding of church and religion.

Revolution and democracy created antagonism toward the conservative currents.

Social, above all economic, equality created antagonism toward the liberal currents.

Social democracy as socialist was above all based on Marxist theory; social democracy was a worker's movement that increasingly came to employ the organizational forms of trade unions and parties. The constitutive element of socialist theory and social democratic practice was in any case the principled opposition to existing social conditions and to the theories legitimating these conditions. Thus, right from its very claim, social democracy had to be perceived as revolutionary, irrespective of the methods social democracy wished to employ to transform the existing society.

The relative uniformity of social democracy concealed an inner diversity, which was expressed at times in vehement arguments among the theorists, sometimes in differing conceptions of the appropriate political strategy. The relative uniformity was possible by virtue of social democracy's absence from power. Behind this homogeneity engendered by powerlessness, there was, in fact, a multiplicity of contradiction. This was grounded in diverse preconditions, differing, for instance, between the United Kingdom and the Continent. It was expressed in the contradiction between Lasalle's position, which was particularly important for Germany, and the main Marxist current as well as in the tension between these main currents and the more syndicalist, anarchist-influenced strains of socialism in Southern and Southwestern Europe. Yet, despite the theoretical diversity, in the second half of the nineteenth century there emerged a largely uniform political instrument, which was also largely understood as being unified: European Social Democracy, an alliance of various workers' parties, consolidated in the Second Socialist International of 1889.[3]

Around the turn of the century European Social Democracy offered a relatively homogenous picture. Standing in the traditions of socialism, chiefly those of the Marxist variety, social democracy was a developed political instrument in all countries, geared to a relatively common goal: consummation of political democracy, fundamental restructuring of the economy, and the establishment of international solidarity. Social democracy was the antithesis of the remnants of political absolutism, of the principles of mature capitalism, and of the egoism of nation-states.

It was not until the fall of social democracy, the breach of the vaunted solidarity that came with the outbreak of war in 1914, that the visible uniformity of European Social Democracy was exposed as the fiction of a movement that, because it was excluded from de facto power, spent itself in resolutions at conferences and congresses. The conduct of European Social Democracy at the beginning of the First World War, together with the ensuing October Revolution, split Social Democracy in Europe and rendered ambiguous the very concept of social democracy within the worker's movement. Since 1914, or 1917, Social Democracy has no longer been synonymous with the worker's movement, no longer synonymous with the practical realization of socialist theory.

In the wake of the October Revolution, the parties attached to the International were splitting everywhere. The concept of socialism was becoming the object of an inheritance dispute between the parties who invoked the traditions of the International in proclaiming the October Revolution and joining together in the Communist International and the parties who likewise stressed the traditions of the International in rejecting the road of the October Revolution. Both socialist currents of tradition called upon the authority of Karl Marx. Yet, the concept of social democracy now became synonymous with rejection of the Soviet road to socialism; with rejection of the Communist variety of socialism; with the at least partial, at least gradual, reconciliation with parliamentarianism, which had originally been denigrated as bourgeois but had in the meantime certainly been democratized. Since the split in the Social Democratic labor movement, social democracy has been synonymous with the socialist movement, which aims to achieve its goals while adhering to the rules of the multiparty system—the framework of Western democracy.

Historically and currently the concept of social democracy contains a certain imprecision. Social democracy can comprise both the theory and the practice of all parties belonging to the Second (the Socialist) International; however, social democracy can at the same time designate those forces within this Inter-

national that can be characterized by a pragmatism of governing,
by a certain abstinence in theory, especially by a break with
the traditions of Marxism. For the Socialist parties of France,
Italy, Spain, Greece, and Portugal (the parties of a "Latin
Socialism" or a "Eurosocialism"), social democracy is not a
concept with which they would identify their theory and practice.
This Mediterranean Socialism feels bound to the International's
parties of the right, to the Social Democracies of Scandinavia,
Germany, the United Kingdom, Austria, and the Benelux countries, which are more familiar with governing power rather than
the concept of democratic socialism. Democratic socialism thus
comprises social democracy in the narrower sense, representing
a type of government socialism and Mediterranean socialism,
which is primarily an opposition socialism. [4]

However, the relative conceptual imprecision holds true
not only for European Social Democracy but also for the other
larger ideological currents and party groupings in Europe. In
order to establish some clarity around the concept of social
democracy and democratic socialism, it is necessary to delineate
the contending concepts in the European political landscape,
concepts that just as much as social democracy and democratic
socialism stand for distinct theoretical traditions and particular
present-day parties.

SOCIAL DEMOCRACY AND BOURGEOIS IDEOLOGIES

In an early phase of modern parliamentarianism, socialist
ideas and Social Democratic parties ruptured the political bi-
polarity that—drawing on the British two-party system from the
seventeenth century—had been established more or less distinctly
in all of Europe. While into the late nineteenth century it was
a matter of course that parliaments, based on unequal suffrage,
were ruled by Conservatives and Liberals, in the wake of the
extension of voting rights the Social Democrats were added as
a third grouping.

Social Democracy was distinguished from the conservative
tendencies and parties by its unqualified advocacy of complete
political democracy. On principle Social Democracy was for the
extension of constitutionalism to a system in which all relevant
constitutional organs were to be directly or indirectly determined
by the people. Of course, Social Democrats were not automatically
republicans, but they were obviously against any monarchy in
which the crown represented an independent power apart from
parliament and the will of the people.

Social Democracy was distinguished from the Liberal tendencies and parties by the postulated bracketing of politics and economics, by the inclusion of economic relations of power in the specifically social democratic conception of democracy. As descendants of the Enlightenment and French Revolution, Social Democrats and Liberals made common cause against the Conservatives, who wanted to carry over and preserve whatever was to be saved from the remnants of feudal authority and legitimacy into the postrevolutionary era. This political alliance between Liberals and Social Democrats had to collapse, however, as soon as the Social Democrats, with their postulate for changing the relations of production, touched the leading interests of the liberal bourgeoisie. The antiaristocratic, antifeudal inclination united Liberals and Social Democrats; social egalitarianism, a part of every form of socialism, had to divide the two currents.[5]

The development of the European democracies in the twentieth century essentially followed the concepts of social democracy. The monarchies were either democratized or abolished, the crown deprived of power on the British or Scandinavian model or else eliminated. Parliamentarianism took root at the heart of the political system, again according to social democratic concepts, based on universal and equal suffrage for women and men regardless of status or class, property or confession, race or education.

However, in the economic realm the European democracies developed only partially in accordance with social democratic concepts. The basic pattern of private property in the means of production remained essentially untouched. Of course, the liberal economics of mature capitalism was surmounted in favor of a social welfare state, and certainly the pressure of the Social Democratic and Communist labor movements worked toward achieving a progressive reform of capitalism; but in none of the states where a free Social Democracy can operate in the twentieth century has there been established a socialist economic order in accordance with the concepts of nineteenth-century social democracy. Rather, Social Democracy has become a lever of permanent reform through the permanent pressure of revolution. To divert the pressure for radical change from a politically powerful worker's movement, the severest consequences of capitalism had to be mitigated and mass misery had to be replaced by social security.

The border line between Social Democracy of the late twentieth century and the bourgeois parties, which continue to be circumscribed by the concepts of liberal and conservative, cannot be as clearly drawn as in the late nineteenth century. The political democracy that is a creation of social democracy is in its essential features (suffrage, parliamentarianism, constitutional liberties) now beyond dispute among Liberal, Conservative, and Social Democratic parties. However, the controversial point remains the jurisdiction of this democracy. Conservatives and Liberals insist that democracy is a political principle that is not to be applied to other social domains, particularly not to the economy. Consistent with their social egalitarianism, Social Democrats stress that democracy (liberty, equality, and fraternity) should not stop at the historically contingent bounds of state and politics. It is not democracy but democracy's jurisdiction that today divides Liberal and Conservative parties on the one hand and Social Democratic and Socialist parties on the other. 6

The discrimination of concepts and parties is, however, fluid. Precisely because political democracy is essentially undisputed among the main bourgeois currents and social democracy and precisely because the rules of democratic distribution of power are observed in the European democracies of 1980, the Liberal and Conservative parties can as ill afford as the Social Democrats to emphasize sharply and clearly their sociopolitical differences. Bourgeois parties must take care that they remain capable of gaining a majority; therefore, they must accept certain minimum concepts of social security as a certain minimum of social equality. Social Democratic parties must also remain capable of winning a majority; hence, they must not alienate the prevailing level of consciousness and they must not frighten off with overdrawn egalitarian demands the strata of voters that are decisive for building a majority. 7

The more stable a multiparty system is, the less can present-day social democracy afford to present an unequivocal socialist concept and thus set itself off from its bourgeois opponents. This consequence of democratic majority rule presents one with difficulty in demarcating social democracy and the bourgeois currents and parties. The partial dissolution of the traditional Liberal and Conservative parties through new types of bourgeois interest representation poses another problem.

For social democracy the shock of the First World War created the initial impulse to split and start anew. For the bourgeois parties the rise of fascism and the beginning of the Second World War was a similarly critical experience. Social democracy was unable to realize its own postulate of international solidarity; in 1914 it broke down into national parties more or less infected with nationalism. Not only were the Liberal and Conservative forces between the world wars unable to stop fascism, but in part they became lackeys of a Mussolini, a Hitler, a Dollfuss, and a Franco. In 1945 they had to start over again. This new beginning is marked by the experiment of a new type of party, the Christian Democratic party.

Established primarily in the Catholic countries of Europe, these parties made and continue to make it difficult to draw a conceptual demarcation between bourgeois and social democratic, for in theory and in practice they affirm and practice elements of the social welfare state much more strongly than the traditional Liberal and Conservative parties. Christian Democracy, precisely in its social policy, converges closely to Social Democratic practice. [8]

The pressure to accommodate that stems from majority rule, the development of Christian Democratic parties as a party type of the decided middle, and the national differences that have never disappeared make it difficult to delineate with conceptual precision the current European landscape of parties. Today it is possible that the Democrazia Christiana of Italy and the Liberal People's party of Sweden advocate restrictions on the market mechanism that the Social Democratic party of Germany rejects. Today it is possible that governing Social Democrats in neutral states or opposition socialists in North Atlantic Treaty Organization (NATO) countries take a foreign policy line that the ruling Social Democrats in NATO countries reject. Programmatic emphasis on theoretical acuity can in no way prevent this practical blurring; one has to count on a certain latitude.

Of course, a countervailing tendency is produced by the need for transnational associations of parties, brought about by direct elections to the European Parliament (EP). The integration of the European Community also leads to an integration of parties, which in this context consistently follow the traditional concepts of Socialists or Social Democrats, Christian Democrats or Conservatives, Liberals, and finally Communists. These traditional associations in the nations of the European Community and in the other countries of Western and Central Europe compel at least an organizational demarcation, drawing the concept of social democracy out of the fog of mere tradition and out of the speculation of sheer programmatics. In the Europe of 1980, social democracy is, at least organizationally, a clearly definable concept behind which there appears a long history and definite sociopolitical aims and objectives. The fluid contours of social democratic practice in no way preclude international contacts and international coordination. Social democracy remains a concept for a minimum of transnational solidarity.

TABLE 1: European Party Federations, 19809

Level:

Level	Communists	Social Democrats	Liberals	Christian Democrats	Conservatives		Fascists
International		Socialist International	Liberal World Union	World Union of Christian Democrats			Eurodestra ("Neofascist International")
European				European Union of Christian Democrats	European Democratic Union+		
European Community		Confederation of the Social Democratic Parties of the EC	Federation of Liberal and Democratic Parties of the EC	European People's Party			
European Parliament	Communist and Allies Group	Socialist Group	Liberal Group	Christian Democratic Group	European Conservative Group	European Progressive Democrats Group++	Unaffiliated Members (MSI-DN)+++
	Communists	Social Democrats	Liberals	Christian Democrats	Conservatives		Fascists

+Founded by conservative parties, by some of the Christian Democratic parties, and by the French Gaullists.
++Consists of French Gaullists, the Irish Fianna Fail, and the Danish Progress party (Glistrup).
+++Unaffiliated is the Italian neofascist MSI-DN (Democrazia Nazionale) and some small parties, most of them of regional character (Scottish Nationalist party, the Flemish Volksunie, the Walloon Francophone Democratic Front), which can by no means be defined as fascists.

SOCIAL DEMOCRACY AND COMMUNISM

All the varieties of social democracy and all the strains of communism originate in the integral worker's movement, which came together in the Socialist International founded in 1889, in the parties united in it, and in the trade unions allied with these parties. These origins in one and the same historical movement are reflected today in the fact that both Social Democratic and Communist parties lay claim to the concept of socialism and to the perceived goal of a socialist social order. The parties of today's Socialist International see themselves as much as forces of the socialist movement as do the Communist parties.

However, this commonality is basically only a verbal one. The practical substance of socialism and the concrete manifestations of socialist society are matters of dispute between Social Democratic and Communist parties. Since the split in the International and with the often hostile competition between the Social Democratic and Communist parties, the following main differences, indeed contradictions, can be observed:

Ideological differences: The Communist parties appeal to the traditions of Marxism and permit no non-Marxist interpretation of socialism; the Social Democratic parties practice an ideological pluralism in which Marxist as well as non-Marxist interpretations of socialism are accepted. [10]

Political differences: Wherever they rule, the Communist parties practice one-party systems without legal opposition; the Social Democratic parties adhere to the rules of the multiparty system wherever they are in power.

Economic differences: Wherever they have been able to institute ruling power, the Communist parties have abolished private property in the means of production in favor of a collective ownership; in their realm of state power the Social Democratic parties have nowhere completely abolished private property but rather have attempted to exert control with the aid of the welfare state postulate.

This conceptual demarcation does not, however, apply in its entirety to the Communist parties that participate legally in the Western multiparty systems. They at least programmatically and verbally observe the rules of party pluralism, accept to some extent non-Marxist ways of thinking in their own ranks, and expressly seek a coexistence of collective and private property. With these Eurocommunist parties the conceptual distinction is not a sharp one. Just as it is no longer possible to delineate sharply and without qualification between the social democracy of today and accommodating bourgeois tendencies, so, too, can there be no unambiguous line of demarcation with such compromising Communist parties.[11]

Of course there remains an ideological, historical, and presently significant difference between social democracy and Eurocommunism. If the notion of communism is to retain any sense, then it implies a fundamental affirmation of the October Revolution and a fundamentally positive estimation of Lenin. Even if the Eurocommunists do not accept the Soviet model for their own areas, even if they criticize the practice of Marxism-Leninism in the "socialist" countries of today, they still assess positively the historic achievement of Marxism-Leninism. If the notion of social democracy or democratic socialism is not to lose all definition, then it, too, implies the historical, ideological rejection of the October Revolution, and it implies a fundamental critique not only of the practice but also of the theory of Lenin.

Thus, between all varieties of democratic socialism and all types of communism there remains as a final, sharp distinction the historical position on the events that brought about the split of the previously integrated Social Democratic worker's movement around 1917. The conception of social democracy at that time (that the socialist revolution could be carried out only by a majority and that it thus was significant only in industrially advanced countries) is today expressed by Social Democracy's consistent defense of democratic rules. Carrying out and legitimating the revolution in an industrially backward country, in which the worker's movement from the start could be based only on a minority, still implies an affirmation (at least with respect to the USSR) of the revolutionary act of foundation, which cannot be justified according to the standards of party pluralism.

The distinction between social democracy and communism has become fluid wherever Communist parties submit to the rules of pluralist democracy and, therefore, are exposed to the same pull toward ideological refinement as were both bourgeois and Social Democratic parties before them. Hence, the ideological, political, and economic differences between social democracy and communism are basically variable and are basically subject to national particularities and historical changes. The conceptual demarcation between the Socialist party and the Communist party in France is not the same as that, say, between the Social Democratic party of Germany and the German Communist party. The position on the USSR constitutes one common differentiation among all Social Democratic (including Eurosocialist) and all

Communist (including Eurocommunist) parties; another is the distinguishing organizational connection. Social Democracy and Eurosocialism mean:

Affiliation with the Socialist International as umbrella organization linking, despite their practical differences, government socialism and opposition socialism;

Rejection of any form of "socialist" one-party system, not only as criticism of concrete relations, but also as a negation on principle.

This final decisive border line can be transcended only when Eurocommunism is social democratized; not only when it practices ideological, political, and economic pluralism as proclaimed in party doctrine, but also when it thoroughly adopts pluralism with regard to the motherland of Communist parties, the USSR. Social democracy is, then, the sum of all forms of socialist movements that aim to achieve their goal of a socialist society, employing solely the methods of pluralist democracy. Communism can credibly link up with this concept of democratic socialism only when it renounces its own hour of birth, the October Revolution.

2
History of Ideas
in Social Democracy

> For many marxists . . . it must at times be difficult
> to know just what is "orthodox" and what is not.
>   C. Wright Mills[1]

Socialism began as a multitude of explanatory models, as
a multitude of ideologies. In France François-Noel Babeuf wanted
to put the watchword equality into practice. For him and the
other early socialists in France, socialism was a political postulate,
the development of political liberalism and at the same time its
antithesis. In the United Kingdom Robert Owen attempted to
change the prevailing economic system through radical reforms
in favor of the exploited. For him and other early British
socialists, socialism was primarily an economic principle, the
development of economic liberalism and at the same time its
antithesis. In Germany there developed a philosophy that—in
spite of its remoteness from practice—depicted history and
society as something changeable (thus, as something changing)
and analyzed faith and religiosity as reflection and escape.[2]

Karl Marx was the first to integrate the various strains of
early socialism. The intellectual history of Social Democracy
had its roots before Marx, but it first really began with Marx.

THE INTEGRAL MARXIST STAGE

Marx and Marxism never constituted a monolithic unity.
Between the young Marx, influenced primarily by German
philosophy, and the old Marx, influenced primarily by British

economics, there existed a tension. Between the Marx of political theory, who aimed to transform a socialist morality into a socialist science, and the Marx of political practice, who was entangled in a web of personal-political trench fights and intrigues, there were contradictions. Karl Marx was a human being and not a theory machine.[3] His life spanned four decades, and certainly no Marxist view of political theory can be so naive as to exclude the changing of fundamental personal and social conditions over such a period from the determining factors of the theory. Despite the multidimensionality in Marx himself, several essential characteristics must be included as part of the store of integral Marxist social democracy.[4]

Historicism: Social development is viewed as the product of definite social formations, the sequence of which is governed by a social regularity. Capitalism follows upon feudalism and is followed by socialism, which is superseded by the final society of communism.

Economism: The succession of steps in social development is determined by the relations of production and the class contradictions conditioned by these relations. The rule of one class over another already bears in itself the future dialectical reversal of class domination by the oppressed.

Revolution: The transition from one form of class rule into another takes place by way of revolution. Of course, this does not necessarily bear the features of terror and the barricades, but the experience of the French Revolution, seen in time-lapse fashion as an historic transfer of power, does exert a considerable exemplary influence on the Marxist understanding of revolution.

Internationalism: The class conflict that moves history forward encompasses the understanding that the working class (as the operative force of social democracy) has to overcome national borders and unite itself. The proletarian has no fatherland to lose, only his chains.

These basic values of Marxist social democracy are to be seen in relation to the previous pre-Marxist, bourgeois, anticlerical, and often antireligious currents of the Enlightenment. Social democracy, even in its integral Marxist phase, was not necessarily antireligious. But it did develop out of the philosophical soil of an ultimately antireligious Enlightenment philosophy, which reached its pinnacle with Ludwig Feuerbach; it did develop from a political soil characterized by the alliance between Throne and Altar, Restoration and Church.

In its integral Marxist stage, social democracy was largely indifferent toward the problem of democracy. What form the socialist revolution would assume, what structures the post-revolutionary socialist society ought to develop, how the legitimation of authority in the transitional stages toward the final communist society might appear, and what the ultimate communist society itself would look like—on these matters Marx himself was essentially silent and social democracy has for the present remained largely quiet.

This indifference toward the problem of democracy is explicable by the absence of democratic structures in the period in which social democracy came into being. The state and society with which early social democracy had to deal was the state of late absolutism and the society of early and mature capitalism. Parliaments were either nonexistent or arenas for the play of interests of a narrow stratum of the upper bourgeoisie. To the extent that early parliamentarianism gave expression to any real social conflicts at all, these conflicts were between the declining feudal aristocracy and the rising bourgeoisie. Nowhere were the interests of the working class legally represented.

This indifference toward democracy was necessarily to become a problem for integral Marxist social democracy as parliamentarianism was increasingly democratized and as liberal freedoms were increasingly extended in such a way that the politically organized worker's movement progressively came to enjoy the possibility of legal activity. It was the economically as well as politically most advanced country, the United Kingdom, that, with its highly developed parliamentarism, deprived social democracy of the historical prerequisites for its democratic abstinence. The relatively highly developed elective franchise and the likewise relatively developed system of social security that the United Kingdom exhibited in the second half of the nineteenth century called for responses other than in the states where elementary political rights first had to be won or secured. The political and economic backwardness of the European Continent made a lasting impression on Marx and the Marxist phase of social democracy; the politically and economically progressive character of the United Kingdom forced a further development of social democratic theory.[5]

The development of British socialism was largely unaffected by the émigré of German extraction who worked in London on his monumental magnum opus for years, indeed decades. No socialist movement in Europe was less Marxist than the British; in the late nineteenth century none encountered such favorable preconditions for a politics that at least in one point contradicted

Godesberg Program signaled a rethinking in the direction of neorevisionism. In its program of 1959, the West German Social Democratic Party (SPD) renounced any clear references to Marxism and accepted the market economy and Western integration. Armed with this theoretical self-image, the SPD resolutely went marching forth into government responsibility. The defeat of West German opposition socialism led first to a theory of government socialism that ultimately made the practice of government socialism possible.[14]

Present-day social democracy is essentially pluralistic. It encompasses parties whose self-images differ at points; these parties are again essentially pluralistic, essentially multifaceted, and even contradictory. The most important tendencies of this current pluralist social democracy are described by the related concepts of government socialism and opposition socialism: government socialism means Social Democracy's abandoning socialist clarity in favor of participation in power, which is of course limited; opposition socialism means Social Democracy's abandoning participation in power in favor of socialist clarity, which of course still does not imply any strategy and tactics for actually transforming society.

These two basic strains are present in every Social Democratic party. Every government socialist party has its tradition of opposition socialism; every opposition socialist party is also potentially government socialist. Without any opposition socialist conscience, government socialism as the priority of strategy over ideology would be devoid of meaning; without any trace of government socialist temptation, opposition socialism as the priority of ideology over strategy would be a sheer confession of faith.[15] Despite this internal dialectic characterizing all parties in the Socialist International, differences in points of emphasis can be discerned today along geographical lines: Social Democracy in those nations bordering on the Mediterranean is rather opposition socialist; Social Democracy in the countries beyond the Mediterranean is rather government socialist.

Yet, this finding captures but the present moment of an active movement. An analysis of Social Democracy 20 years from now, at the turn of the century, will perhaps bring substantially different results. Austrian Social Democracy affords an example of a shift in emphasis. Between the founding of the republic in 1918 and the civil war in 1934, the Austro-Marxist party in its politics and theory was a model example of the attempt to remain true to Marxist roots a good 50 years after Marx's death. The consistent opposition role that Austrian Social Democracy played or had to play from 1920 on was closely

TABLE 2: From Marxism of the Late 19th Century to Social Democracy of the Late 20th Century[16]

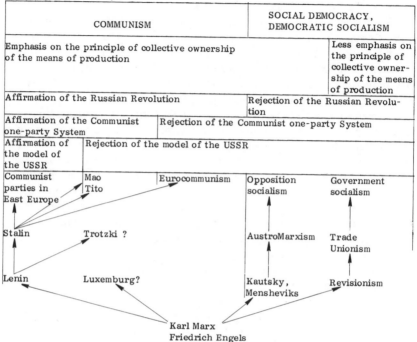

related to its Austro-Marxist theory. By the same token, the change of Austrian opposition socialism to a government socialism was causally linked to the change of the Austrian Socialist party (SPÖ) to an almost permanent party in power. With a total of 31 years in the government between 1945 and 1980 (21 years as coalition partner, 10 years as sole party in power), the opposition socialist consciousness expressed in the party program was gradually transformed into a government socialist consciousness, likewise caste in a program form. The party programs of the years 1958 and 1978 were the theoretical culmination of a practical change, an expression of the flexibility that even Social Democracy, with its programmatic tradition, has to develop if it wants not only to analyze society but also to shape it.

Social Democracy is in flux. In 1981 the British Labour party, one of the rich-traditioned parties of the Socialist International and a classic model of government socialism, was split. Of course, it necessarily remains an open question whether the newly founded Social Democratic party of the United Kingdom, whose acceptance into the Socialist International is initially not possible because of the Labour party's opposition, will alter the British two-party system and, thus, decisively influence the role of Social Democracy. With the triumphal electoral victory of the Socialist party of France in 1981, in the framework of the Socialist International it came to represent almost the ideal type of opposition socialist party. It remains open whether this change of roles for French Social Democracy will also entail a change of its action. The 1981 election victory of Greek Socialism (PASOK), which, although not a member of the Socialist International for reasons of foreign policy, nevertheless can have a not inconsiderable influence on the future of socialism in Southern Europe. Finally, in 1981 the preliminary decisions were made for Spain's entry into NATO, whereby it remains open whether the country's largest opposition party, the Socialist International member Socialist Workers' party (PSOE) would give up its original objections to admission to NATO.

Social democracy is in flux. So is the society from which it emerges, which it has wanted to change, has in fact partially changed, and represents by virtue of that very change. The equally vigorous and many-sided—indeed explosively contradictory—development that Marxism has undergone in the one century since Karl Marx shows its vitality. Karl Marx stands today for movements and parties that in part struggle against one another, that excommunicate one another from the respective "orthodox" churches of their own special Marxism, that neither in theory nor in practice constitute a unity. Only a political theory that is remote from the levers of concrete power and is not at all interested in realizing its claims can in the long run allow itself an unequivocal demand, a purity of doctrine, and a uniformity of organization without giving consideration to the needs of power. Social democracy today is many things—but it is most certainly not in principle averse to power. Social democracy aims at political practice.

3
Development of Social Democratic and Socialist Parties

> It is a fairly common occurrence that reformist or
> revolutionary parties become conservative once the
> reforms or revolutions they have fought for are
> accomplished: they move from the Left to the Right.
> Maurice Duverger[1]

In its integral Marxist stage, social democracy aimed to
represent the working class. It organized the worker's movement
as a party and as a trade union. As a union the Social Democratic worker's movement was closely linked with the party—in
the United Kingdom even ahead of the party, on the Continent
connected like a "Siamese twin."[2] As a party Social Democracy
followed a relatively uniform pattern. Social Democratic parties
prior to 1914 constituted a quite specific type of political party.
They were either mass parties, class parties, or integration
parties.

As mass parties, they distinguished themselves from the
Conservative and Liberal parties through their claim to be more
than associations for nominating candidates and organizing electoral campaigns. They also saw themselves as organizations that
had to carry out political education independent of general elections; that had to win over as many supporters as possible as
members and, thus, secure an autonomous financial base; that
could in this way challenge the bourgeois parties of notables,
which were run on an amateur basis, by means of a professionally
run apparatus.

As class parties, they distinguished themselves from their
opponents through their claim of representing exclusively or

primarily the interests of a particular group, namely the working class. The goal of Social Democratic parties was not some common good, behind which Social Democracy suspected the ideologically veiled interest of the ruling class, but the good of the working class. Even if nonproletarians, in particular intellectuals, always had an important role in Social Democracy, still the self-image and daily experience of Social Democratic parties was fundamentally proletarian, and that meant as much antiaristocratic as antibourgeois.

As an integration party, Social Democracy distinguished itself from the various types of bourgeois parties through the claim not only of encompassing its supporters in the narrower, political sense but also of organizing all facets of their social existence (ultimately, all areas of their lives). Social Democratic parties were surrounded with a field or organizations that were not directly part of the party but were linked to the party: trade unions, youth organizations, old people's organizations, sports clubs, student groups, and so forth. A Social Democratic party was like a camp, a specifically proletarian subculture.[3]

HISTORICAL TURNING POINTS

Behind this typological uniformity of Social Democratic parties there stood a commonality—the commonly shared distance from the levers of state power and from the principles of the social order. Social Democracy was an antithesis; it was also organized as conscious opposition to the prevailing understanding of politics, parties, and representation.

The problems of party typology were never simply tactical or even formal questions. The decisive turning points in the general development of social democracy were therefore also turning points for Social Democracy as a definite type of political party. These turning points were an emphatically sharp demarcation vis-à-vis Communist parties and an increasingly sharp demarcation vis-à-vis Liberal, Conservative, and Christian Democratic parties.

Social Democracy's opting for democracy in the form of a multiparty system promoted its permeability against the bourgeois parties, but it also promoted a sharp delineation from the Communist parties. The features of integral Marxist social democracy changed accordingly. It clearly drew back from the Communist cadre party; the mass party became an open, mass membership party and an equally open mass electoral party. In the train of rivalry with the bourgeois parties and the accommodation

forced by it, the class party became a people's party that in no
way wanted to restrict its claim to representation solely to the
proletariat. Finally, favored by the drawing force of the multiparty system, the integration party became a catchall party
that replaced the tendency toward a dogmatic surrogate church
with the tendency toward secularized optionality.

A precedent, the significance of which was at first not at
all recognized, emerged at the party congress of Russian Social
Democracy in exile in 1903. Lenin's advocacy of the principle
of a vanguard party of cadre and his inner party opponents'
insistence on the principle of the mass party provoked the split
of Russian Social Democracy into a majority wing (Bolsheviks)
and a minority wing (Mensheviks). Thus, the division in the
Social Democratic worker's movement, which was finally to come
about in 1917, was already foreshadowed in 1903, brought about
by a dispute over a problem that at first glance appeared to be
an organizational problem of secondary importance. [4]

However, there were differing conceptions of strategy
behind this conflict, and again differing conceptions of democracy
became apparent. Should the revolution be advanced by a
minority that saw itself as the vanguard of the worker's movement and that wanted to derive its legitimation from an advanced
level of consciousness? Or should not the revolution rather be
the concern of the entire proletariat, which was gradually and
automatically becoming the majority, such that the revolution
should become possible (indeed, a matter of course) according
to the basic idea of the bourgeois principle of majority rule?

Here is the conception of a party that knows better than
those actually concerned what is good for them; there is the
conception of a party that classifies itself as merely a reflection
of the level of consciousness of those affected. Here is the
inclination to anticipate the revolution by the intervention of a
revolutionary elite; there is the inclination to neglect the revolution through constant waiting. The Bolsheviks—and in their
wake the Communist parties—were infected by the danger of
putschism; the Mensheviks—and in their wake the Social Democratic parties—were plagued by the danger of a wait-and-see
attitude. [5]

Of course, in the illegal struggle against absolutist regimes—
such as czarist Russia—the Social Democratic mass party was at
a disadvantage compared with the Communist cadre party. However, in the legal exchange of the advanced systems of Western
Europe, the mass party clearly had the advantage. In the
countries that were coming around to parliamentary democracy
(such as the United Kingdom, France, Germany, Austria-Hungary,

and Italy), the conspiratorial element of party cadre and professional revolutionaries was not necessary. The mass party provided a broad base in two respects: an agitational base and a financial base.

Through broad organizational work, increasing numbers of voters could be turned into sympathizers, more and more sympathizers could become members, and more and more members could become activists. The large number of members also helped provide Social Democracy with at least a portion of its means in the form of regular membership dues, monies that its bourgeois opponents received in the form of generous donations from aristocrats and industrialists.

The superiority of mass parties over cadre parties in the legal struggle within a parliamentary multiparty system was also confirmed decades after the historic split of 1903; the fact is that Communist parties that are fully exposed to the competitive struggle of the multiparty system have been forced to give up the organizational principle of the cadre party. The phenomenon of Eurocommunism has been characterized by the substitution of a functional alternative model for the Leninist party type, which was recognized to be anachronistic and dysfunctional.

Both mass party and the battleground of legality and mass party and open party rivalry go hand in hand in the history of social democracy. Thus organized, social democracy in many cases became acquainted with governing power after the First World War—in the United Kingdom, Germany, France, and some smaller nations. Originally distanced from state and society, social democracy came in this way to the centers of state and society. This change from principled opposition to partial identification with existing conditions necessarily precipitated a change in party type. A party that assumes government responsibility cannot be completely distanced in confronting the order over which this government rules. A party that governs must also gradually reexamine its alternative subculture, change it, and adapt it.

The Social Democratic parties that first and most intensively were to partake of state power were also the first to alter their character as a class party and as an integration party in a step-by-step fashion; in part they became people's parties or catchall parties.

That a worker's party was governing, that a worker's party was reforming, and that a worker's party was bringing distinct improvements in the way of social security and in the form of social position promoted the reconciliation of the worker's movement with the existing conditions. The gulf between the ruling order and the worker's movement was at least psychologically overcome by nothing so much as the successes of Social Democracy.

This reconciliation effect of government socialism was strengthened by general social tendencies. To be sure, the class of those dependent upon wage labor had become, as Marx predicted, the overwhelming majority in all advanced societies; however, within this class there developed differences in status and consciousness. The most important form of this differentiation was the only partially mediated coexistence of blue-collar and white-collar workers. Within the majority class of non-self-employed, white-collar workers became increasingly numerous and important. [6]

Partial reconciliation of the proletariat with the existing conditions and partial ascendancy of those strata in the proletariat with less of a footing in a consciously proletarian tradition—these circumstances forced a Social Democracy that had to win elections for the sake of realizing its goals to adapt its structure as well. It could no longer be a class party like that of 1900; it could no longer be an integration party that satisfied not just the social and economic needs of its followers but their secondary religious needs as well. It had to become a party based on more than the workers (in the narrower sense), one that could win over the white-collar workers in particular; it had to become a party offering as much as possible to as many as possible, becoming stratified and pluralistic, and glittering and ambiguous.

Precisely those Social Democratic parties that are particularly successful in the legal democratic struggle for power against their Liberal, Conservative, and Christian Democratic opponents are subject to this process of adaptation. They can have nothing but success, because they also adapt to existing relations in their outward characteristics; the more success they have, the less reason their followers have to feel like proletarians from the turn of the century. The stronger a Social Democracy becomes, the more its followers have to lose.

The development of Social Democratic parties is thus subject to an inescapable dialectic: their success is paid for by softening up their distinctive socialist cast; their firm socialist profile is paid for by diminishing prospects of success. Government socialism as the quintessence of successful socialism has entered into a symbiosis with the prevailing relations, relations it has changed and through which it has changed. The parties of government socialism must therefore be particularly well adapted in their outward form; they must be particularly far removed from the origins of social democracy. [7]

TABLE 3: Workers' Percentage of Voters of Social Democratic Parties [8]

Country of Social Democratic or Socialist Parties	Voters (in percent)		
	Workers (blue collar)	Civil Servants, Employees (white collar)	Employers, Nonemployed Professions
Austria (1969)	68	25	7
Belgium (1968)	61	24	16
Denmark (1971)	71	25	4
Germany (1967)	61	32	8
Finland (1966)	74	26	
France (1965)	43	25	32
Italy - PSI (1958)	76	24	
Italy - PSDI (1958)	41	59	
Norway (1965)	66	22	12
Sweden (1968)	67	26	7
United Kingdom (1966)	71	29	

Some of the newer data already available about the composition of the social democratic electorate has not been used, because it was not possible to integrate these data into the methodology of social measurement Raschke has developed.

Of course, a look at the social structure of Social Democratic parties of the present shows that a dichotomy between a surely powerful and ideologically amorphous people's or catchall party and a surely powerless but sharply defined class party is unrealistic. Precisely those parties in which opposition socialism and a stress on the class character of the party are predominant have a smaller proportion of workers among their supporters, and the parties representative of the priority of government socialism and the popular character of the party represent a larger proportion of workers.

Socialist parties that emphatically define themselves as class parties are in reality hardly worker's parties at all any more. Social Democratic parties that have largely given in to the trend toward the people's party are still, in their rank-and-file bases, more strongly identifiable as worker's parties. This paradox is a consequence of the fact that opposition Socialist parties normally confront very strong Communist parties, which have won over and thus drawn away from Social Democracy a large proportion (often the majority) of the workers, while government Socialist parties usually have no larger Communist parties to their left and frequently have a near monopoly on the votes of the workers.

This contradictoriness between claim and reality shows the nature of modern Social Democratic parties in general: their theory and their programs are a part of a reality that scarcely reflects or determines the other parts (electorate, membership, or political activity). Social Democratic parties, which theoretically are preserving the tradition of the proletarian class party, are in reality quite far removed from this tradition. In the realm of party typology, the distance between theory and practice is even more pronounced in the case of the parties of opposition socialism than with the parties of government socialism.

Opposition socialism, characterized by programmatic and typological traditionalism, has not achieved power and has lost the workers; government socialism, with its programmatic and typological opportunism, has gained power and carried the workers.

TENDENCIES IN THE SOCIAL DEMOCRATIC PARTY TYPOLOGY

Otto Kirchheimer has used the example of the Social Democratic parties of Europe to describe the development of the catchall type of party he defines. In so doing he distinguishes three

stages:[9] the period of the party's steady growth, roughly up
to 1914; the period of initial experience in governmental responsibility, between the world wars; and the period of opening up
to all sectors of the population, after 1945.

The third stage encompasses the transition from mass,
class, and integration party to the present type of Social Democratic party. Social democracy has Americanized itself, taking
on the following characteristics: a retreat from ideology through
giving priority to short-term tactics over long-term strategy;
personality politics through concentrating party activity on a
few leading politicians; devaluation of the party member to a
regular paying voter; orientation not to the class but to the
general public; and contacts with business associations of
various interests.

These defining characteristics of a catchall party are to
be understood as partially examined, partially verified hypothesis. A comparative, complete description of Social Democratic
parties must face the challenge of this central hypothesis formulated in the way of a catalog. What do Social Democratic parties
claim to be? Do they wish to be class parties or people's parties?
What sort of organizational goal do they pursue? Does this goal
remain oriented to the objectives of a mass party? To what
extent do Social Democratic parties represent a still secondary
world view? Do they give themselves the character of parties
with partial philosophies?

It can be taken as certain that the departure from the
traditional type has been partially or largely completed. It is
equally certain that this further development has taken place
in the most varied ways. But what conditions have produced
the Social Democratic catchall parties, with their largely plurialis-
tic ideology? What conditions effect the national differences
between an opposition Socialist party (such as the Italian Socialist
party [PSI]) and a government Socialist party (such as the West
German Social Democratic party [SPD])? To what extent can
we still speak of a definite type of Social Democratic party at all?
Answers to these questions can be sought in the areas of the
internal structure, external relations, and the self-image of
Social Democratic parties.

If we accept Giovanni Sartori's division of party systems
into simple pluralism, moderate pluralism, and extreme pluralism,
then the position of Social Democracy in Western and Central
Europe in 1980 is fairly clear.[10] In the simple pluralist party
systems, which are bipolar, nonpolarized, and centripetal,
Social Democracy is always basically one of the two poles, such
as in the United Kingdom. With moderate pluralist systems,

TABLE 4: Degree of Concentration of the European Party
Systems and Strength of Social Democratic Parties,
about 1980[13]

Party, Year of General Election	Votes (in percent)	Number of Parties with More Than 3 Percent
Austria/SPÖ (1979)	51.0	3
Sweden/SAP (1979)	43.5	5
Germany/SPD (1980)	42.9	3
United Kingdom/Lab (1979)	37.8	3
France/PS (1981)[+]	37.5	4
Norway/A (1981)	37.2	7
Denmark/S (1981)	37.1	7
Spain/PSOE (1979)	30.5	4
Netherlands/PvdA (1981)	28.3	4
Belgium/BSP/PSB (1977)	27.4	5[++]
Portugal/PS (1980)[+++]	27.1	3
Switzerland/SPS (1979)	24.9	6
Finland/SDP (1979)	24.0	8
Italy/PSI and PSDI (1979)	13.6	7

[+]Together with a small left-liberal group Mouvement des
Radicaux de Gauche (MRG), results of the second ballot.

[++]The separation of the christian-democratic, socialist and
liberal blocs, according to the ethnic borders, has not been
considered.

[+++]Together with two small groups.

which are also bipolar and centripetal but partially polarized,
Social Democracy is here again one of the two poles or else
dominates in one of the poles, such as in France. Only in
extreme pluralist systems, which are multipolar, polarized, and
centrifugal, does Social Democracy threaten to become a force
of the third order, as in Italy.

In any case, it does seem to be a fact that, with a growing
concentration in the party system, Social Democracy gains in
importance and that, with a decreasing concentration, it loses
importance. An unambiguous situation of competition is mani-
festly favorable for Social Democracy; a many-layered, many-
sided situation of competition, on the other hand, is evidently
unfavorable.

If we accept Jean Blondel's division of party systems into two, two-and-a-half, and multiparty systems[11], then this conclusion is basically confirmed. Social Democracy is nowhere in danger of being overtaken by a trend to the two-party system; basically it stands to benefit from such a development in every case, for in such concentrated systems it is always the dominant party on the left. With the fragmentation of the party system, the significance of the Communist parties as well as that of the left Socialist splinter parties grows out of proportion.[12] With growing concentration, the strength of Social Democracy likewise increases disproportionately.

4
Structure of
Social Democratic and
Socialist Parties

Consideration for the newly integrated or newly recruited elements, the fellow travellers, who are still far removed from the world of socialist or democratic ideas, does, however, make the conduct of principled politics immediately prohibitive.

Robert Michels[1]

Present-day social democracy is alive in various political parties engaged in open rivalry with other parties, generally in countries that are highly developed economically. Of course, a relatively uniform type of Social Democratic or Socialist party has taken shape only in Europe; analyses of the internal structure of Social Democracy concentrate on this type.

At the center there are the following parties belonging to the Socialist International:[2]

Austria - Socialist party (SPÖ)
Belgium - Socialist party (BSP/PSB)
Denmark - Social Democratic party (S)
Federal Republic of Germany - Social Democratic party (SPD)
Finland - Social Democratic party (SPD)
France - Socialist party (PS)
Italy - Socialist party (PSI)
      - Social Democratic party (PSDI)
Netherlands - Labor party (PvdA)
Norway - Labor party (A)
Portugal - Socialist party (PS)
Spain - Socialist Workers' party (PSOE)

Sweden - Social Democratic Workers party (SAP)
Switzerland - Social Democratic party (SPS)
United Kingdom - Labour party (Lab)

Not included in the analysis is the large Socialist party of
Greece, the Pan-Hellenic Socialist Movement (PASOK), which
does not belong to the Socialist International. Only marginally
considered are the Social Democratic and Socialist parties of
the smaller states of Europe: the Labour party of Ireland, which
is traditionally the third strongest party in the country; the
Social Democratic party of Iceland, which is only fourth among
the island's parties; the Socialist Workers' party of Luxembourg,
which is the second of three relatively large parties; the Labour
party of Malta, which has been the party in power in this two-
party system for quite some time; the Social Democratic and
Labour party of Northern Ireland, the leading representative
of the Catholic sector of the population; and the Labour party
of Northern Ireland, which plays only a minority role within
the Protestant element in Northern Ireland.[3]

ELECTORATE AND MEMBERSHIP

The voters and the members of a party constitute the two
external, concentric circles around the core of party leaders
and functionaries. Every party needs voters; participating in
elections and winning over voters are defining characteristics
of a political party. Every modern party also needs members.
With the end of the nineteenth century parties of notables,
members have become an obvious intermediate level linking the
nonbinding loyalty of the voter and the particular activity of
the party official by means of a binding though rather passive
loyalty.
    It was mainly the Social Democratic worker's parties that
created the type of mass membership party. As representative
of the socially weak, Social Democracy sought to create a financial equalizer to the bourgeois parties by means of a mass organization of its followers; moreover, it saw the tightest possible
network of members as a chance for developing political consciousness and mobilizing. Following the split with the Bolsheviks
and their fundamentally different type of organization, Social
Democracy plainly constituted the membership parties.

Direct and Indirect Organization

The inclusion of members assumed various forms in particular Social Democratic parties. The two basic models of organizational structure, which began to take shape early on, are still current today. Alongside the dominant direct structure, some Social Democratic parties also show an indirect structure.[4]

Direct structure means that a party's membership can be acquired exclusively by the admission of individuals. The auxiliary membership of grass roots organizations and groups closely associated with the party can certainly complement the party membership proper but cannot replace it.

Indirect structure means that the party membership is established by means of membership in an organization closely connected with a party, in a particular association. Admission to the party does not take place directly with the party organization itself but rather indirectly with some intermediary grass roots, subsidiary, or affiliated organization interconnected with the party.

Of the large Social Democratic parties, the British Labour party, the Norwegian Labor party, and the Swedish Social Democratic party exhibit an indirect structure, as does the Labour party of the Republic of Ireland. Individual membership is possible, but the number of members admitted directly is generally (in the United Kingdom, Sweden, and Ireland, but not in Norway) smaller than the number of indirect members.

Indirect membership expresses a definite relationship between Social Democracy and trade unions: unions that establish for their members a kind of collective membership in a Social Democratic party, and parties that in this way do not have to win a large proportion of their members on an individual basis but get them indirectly through the unions. There are several special features behind this: an historical precedence of the unions over the parties (the United Kingdom and Ireland); a particularly strong position of the unions in the political system (the United Kingdom and the Scandinavian countries); a traditional political synchronization between Social Democracy and Social Democratic-oriented unions; and a trade unionist tradition in Social Democracy and thus a traditional priority of government socialism over opposition socialism.

The indirect structure is most strongly pronounced with the British Labour party, where it has its deepest roots. The British Labour party consists of four subsidiary organizations: the trade union section, which furnishes almost 90 percent of the membership; the electoral district section, which organizes

TABLE 5: Social Democratic Parties with Indirect Structure[5]

	Labour party United Kingdom (1974)	Labour party Ireland (1977)[+]	Labor party Norway (1976)[++]	SAP Sweden (1977)[+]
Individual members	691,889	8,000	93,557	300,000
Collective members (unions)	5,787,467	200,000	50,377	800,000
Collective members (others)	39,101[+++]	–	–	–

[+]Estimated.

[++]Exact figures for total membership only, distinction between individual and collective members, estimated.

[+++]Cooperative movements as well as Fabian Socialist Societies.

the individual members and provides roughly 10 percent; and the sections of the cooperative movement as well as the Fabian and Socialist societies, which have essentially only historical significance and altogether supply less than 1 percent of all members.[6]

The predominance of the indirect union membership is fully revealed at the party conferences (annual congresses) of the Labour party. Because the membership figures are expressed directly in delegate votes and since the representatives of the unions vote in blocks, the trade unions dominate the annual party conferences. In the party executive, on the other hand, the unions are guaranteed only a 40 percent share, and so here the nonunion interests and groupings find the possibility of forming an alternative majority.

After many decades of contention with the other parties, the relationship between the unions and the Labour party has been governed since 1946 by collective membership, with the possibility of individual withdrawal. Every union member is automatically a party member unless released from the collective membership by a unilateral individual declaration. However, the majority of union members accept the collective membership; the possibility of separating union membership and party membership is only rarely made use of. The close intertwining of trade unions and Social Democracy in the form of collective, indirect membership has financial as well as historical causes. The financial strength of the Labour party relies mainly on the close relationship of the party to the trade unions.

The intertwining of unions and Social Democracy at the level of the membership is less pronounced with the Social Democratic parties of Sweden and Norway. In these two Scandinavian countries, separate trade union organizations must pass their own resolutions on admission to the party; a domination of the party conferences by trade union voting blocks is not possible. In this way the indirect character of the party structure is less prominent in the Swedish and Norwegian Social Democratic parties than in the British Labour party.[7]

The unmediated, direct structure is the normal case of Social Democratic organization. The parties build upon the principle of the local branch (section), which differs from the traditional bourgeois principle of the caucus and from the traditional Communist principle of the cell in several ways.[8] The local branch makes a relatively narrow geographical aspect the foundation of party organization; the caucus is a rather loose, geographically broad association of notables; the cell places a narrow professional solidarity at the center of the organization.

These differences in the construction of the direct party structures are, however, no longer as marked as they were a few decades ago. As the major European parties, regardless of their bourgeois, Social Democratic, or Communist origins, have clearly developed in the direction of the people's and catchall party, a rather loosely interpreted local branch principle has come into general acceptance beyond the confines of the Social Democratic parties. The organizational feature of social democracy historically has become the organizational feature of European parties in general.

At the membership level, the directly structured parties are also strongly influenced by the existence of intraparty divisions, groups, and grass roots organizations. The trend toward the people's party has led Social Democratic parties to call into being for particular target groups organizations that seem particularly well suited to link representatives of such groups to the party.

The working groups of the SPD are one example of this form of target group, where specific membership structure is linked into a directly structured party. The West German Social Democrats (SPD) have founded within the party special organizations in which party members automatically possess membership by virtue of specific criteria. Membership in the subsidiary

organization (working group) follows party membership; in the
indirectly structured parties, on the other hand, party membership follows membership in an extra-party organization (trade
unions). In 1978 in the SPD the following organizations were
instituted for specific party members: [9]

Working Group for Young Socialists
Working Group for Social Democrats in the Field of Education
    (encompassing the former Working Group of Social Democratic
    Teachers)
Working Group of Social Democratic Women
Working Group for Labor Questions
Working Group of the Self-Employed in the SPD
Working Group of Social Democrats in the Field of Health Services
    (encompassing the former Working Group of Social Democratic
    Doctors and Pharmacists)
Working Group of Social Democratic Lawyers

This inclination of Social Democracy to approach the different groups of members differently according to specific criteria
is an acknowledgment that a Social Democratic membership party,
with a consistently unmediated structure, no longer represents
the optimum in organizing. An undifferentiated Social Democratic
party that wants to address all voters solely as Social Democrats
reaches a smaller number than a party that aims to and can
address Social Democratic women specifically as women, Social
Democratic intellectuals specifically as intellectuals, or Social
Democratic tradesmen specifically as tradesmen. This arrangement is also a sign of the turn away from the class party typical
of social democracy in its integral Marxist stage.

Thus, today the organizational structure of Social Democratic parties is predominantly that of the basic model of a direct,
unmediated membership party, building through individual
membership. At the same time this typically Social Democratic
membership party (in most cases unmediated) is highly differentiated and departmentalized; in its structure of membership and
in the very breadth of organization it offers members, it mirrors
the actual and desired diversity of modern social democracy.

Overall Strength and Organizational Texture

The rise of the Social Democratic parties is confirmed by
every comparison of European party systems; Social Democratic
parties are without exception major parties. In all the party

systems of Western and Central Europe, the Social Democrats are either the strongest vote-getting party or the second strongest. Only in Italy are they the third strongest party. Alongside the Christian Democratic and Conservative parties, the Social Democrats are the leading political force among parties.

The leading role of Social Democratic parties is somewhat less pronounced when membership figures are compared. A few exceptionally well-organized bourgeois parties (such as the Finnish Center party or the Austrian People's party) have, despite lower voter figures, surpassed their Social Democratic rivals in the number of members. Of course, European Social Democracy is also a leading force at the membership level; however, the Social Democratic parties no longer represent the model case of a tightly organized member party, although in an earlier phase of development they were the first to have put the type of membership party into practice at all.

This becomes all the more clear when one takes into account the indirect structure of the British Labour party and the Swedish and Norwegian Social Democratic parties. If only individual membership were considered, then the advantage that these three parties show in terms of membership would be smaller or—in the case of the United Kingdom—make the Conservatives the party with the largest membership.

The membership type of party is also characterized by the fact that the number of supporters organized as members is particularly high in relation to the total number of the party's voters. In comparative studies of parties, the percentage of members of a party to voters (degree of organization) is considered an important indicator of the organizational strength of a party. In the European context it is striking that the Social Democratic parties fare significantly less well in comparisons of this relative dimension of degree of organization than in comparisons of the two absolute quantities of number of voters and number of members.

The grouping of Social Democratic parties into those showing a government socialist emphasis and those with a preponderance of opposition socialism shows a definite coherence. In general, the government Socialist parties are stronger than the opposition Socialist parties both in numbers of voters and in numbers of members. While the majority of government Socialist parties consists of parties with the greatest electoral strength and roughly half of the government Socialist parties includes parties with the largest membership, among the opposition Socialist parties only one has the greatest voting strength and not one has the largest membership. However, the order in terms of

TABLE 6: Strength of Social Democratic Parties on the
National Level—Voters, Members, and
Organizational Degree[10]

	Position of the Social Democratic Party in the National Party System			Communist Voters above 10 Percent
	Voters[+]	Members[++]	Organizational Degree[++]	
Parties with emphasis on government socialism				
Austria (SPÖ)	1	2	2	no
Belgium (BSP/PSB)	2	2	2	no
Denmark (S)	1	1	3	no
Finland (SDP)	1	2	2	yes
Germany (SPD)	2	1	1	no
Great Britain (Lab)	2	1[+++]	1	no
Netherlands (PvdA)	2	2	4	no
Norway (A)	1	1[+++]	3	no
Sweden (SAP)	1	1[+++]	1	no
Switzerland (SPS)	1	3	3	no
Parties with emphasis on opposition socialism				
France (PS)	1	4	4	yes
Italy (PSI)	3	3	2	yes
(PSDI)	5	5	1	yes
Portugal (PS)	2	2	2	yes
Spain (PSOE)	2	2	2	yes

[+]For details, see Table 4.
[++]See Table 7.
[+++]Individual and collective membership, see Table 5.

Note: Only those parties are included that are represented in the national parliament; splinter parties are not part of the comparison.

degree of organization has no discernible connection with the government or opposition socialism classification.

The fact that government Socialist parties operate from a position of relative strength while opposition Socialist parties often work from a position of relative weakness must also be seen in the context of rivalry with a strong Communist party. Since left socialist tendencies do not represent any real order of magnitude, the Communist parties are the only important competition for Social Democratic parties in the realm of the traditional left. It is the Communist parties that can contend with Social Democracy for the leading position on the left of the political party spectrum. Opposition socialism and the relative strength of Communism are as interrelated as opposition socialism and the relative weakness of Social Democracy.

Naturally, comparing membership figures of different parties can give us only approximate values. The concept of membership is different from one party to the next. Differences exist not only between direct and indirect membership but also among the different varieties of unmediated, direct membership. Thus, the Radical Democratic party of Switzerland (RDP) counts among its members those sympathizers who attend party meetings only occasionally and by no means make regular contributions; the Social Democratic party of Switzerland (SPS), on the other hand, considers as members only those who regularly pay party dues. This results in an advantage of the RDP over the SPS in terms of degree of organization. 11

A like comparison is of course easier to make between the different Social Democratic parties; still it must be borne in mind that even the various parties of the Socialist International interpret the concept of membership with differing degrees of liberality. The following comparison of membership figures and degree of organization of the parties must be given this qualification. Nevertheless, this comparison does furnish some indication of the very diverse organizational strengths of the individual parties of European Social Democracy and of their abilities to bind supporters to the party and turn uncommitted sympathy into committed membership.

The degree of organization of the individual parties tends to be declining. This tendency can be derived from the tabulations that Maurice Duverger made for the late 1950s. Most Social Democratic parties—in the Federal Republic of Germany, Denmark, France, Norway, and Austria—exhibit 30 years later a significantly lesser degree of organization. However, in many of these cases this cannot be attributed to a decline in membership but rather to an increase in the number of voters,

TABLE 7: Strength of Membership and Organizational Degree
of Social Democratic Parties[12]

	Members[+]	Organizational Degree[++] (in percent)
Austria (SPÖ)	703,624 (1976)	29
Belgium (BSP/PSB)	255,000 (1977)	17
Denmark (S)	123,000 (1975)	12
Finland (SDP)	101,000 (1975)	15
France (PS)	200,000 (1977)	2
Germany (SPD)	1,021,000 (1977)	6
Italy (PSI)	665,000 (1978)	19
(PSDI)	300,000 (1978)	24
Netherlands (PvdA)	145,000 (1970)	6
Norway (A)	143,934 (1976)[+++]	16
Portugal (PS)	96,000 (1976)	6
Spain (PSOE)	150,000 (1977)	3
Sweden (SAP)	1,100,000 (1976)[+++]	47
Switzerland (SPS)	55,000 (1975)	11
United Kingdom (Lab)	6,518,457 (1974)[+++]	64

[+]Data following in some cases only global or estimated figures given by the parties.

[++]For the elections indicated in Table 4.

[+++]Individual and collective membership.

with which the development of membership has not been able to keep pace.

In any case, in both areas of investigation the Social Democratic parties of the United Kingdom, Austria, and Sweden yield the top values. In their organizational structure these three parties are completely different: in the British Labour party the mediated structure is dominant; in the Swedish Social Democratic party the direct and indirect structures are of approximately equal strength; and in the SPÖ there exists only a direct organizational form. Yet, for all three parties the priority of government socialism is typical; after 1945 all three parties have held office over many years (in Sweden and Austria for most of that time). In addition, the United Kingdom, Sweden, and Austria can be considered particularly highly developed social welfare states; in each country there is a tightly organized, strong, certainly cooperatively disposed trade union movement, interrelated with Social Democracy in various ways.

TABLE 8: Comparative Organizational Degree of Social Democratic Parties, Late 1940s and Late 1970s[13]

	Organizational Degree[++] (in percent)	
	Late 1940s	Late 1970s
United Kingdom (Lab)[+]	43 (1949-50)	64 (1974)
Sweden (SAP)[+]	36 (1948)	47 (1976)
Austria (SPÖ)	38 (1949)	29 (1978)
Norway (A)[+]	26 (1949)	16 (1976)
Denmark (S)	35 (1950)	12 (1975)
Switzerland (SPS)	22 (1947)	11 (1975)
Netherlands (PvdA)	10 (1948)	6 (1970)
Germany (SPD)	9 (1949)	6 (1977)
France (SFIO, PS)	8 (1946)	2 (1977)

[+]Individual and collective membership.
[++]For details, see Table 7.

With their fundamentally unchanged, leading position among
voters in the European multiparty systems, the rather decreasing
organizational density of Social Democratic parties once again
points to social democracy's tendency toward accommodation.
Following its beginnings as the prototype of a membership party
and parallel to its long-term increasing significance for the
power structure of precisely the most developed countries of
Europe, Social Democracy has partially taken on the features
of a less tightly organized electoral party. Where membership
in a Social Democratic party can be acquired only by individual
admissions, the percentage of Social Democratic members to
Social Democratic voters tends to decrease.

The Social Democratic parties of Europe have also become
in terms of structure (related to the external spheres of participation in the form of voting and joining) parties of the prevailing
normality. A part of this normality is that the party of notables
has indeed had its day, but the membership party has simultaneously been eroded. In view of the party leadership's dependence
on winning elections and, thus, on particular strata of voters,
the individual member has to become less important in the party
hierarchy. When in doubt, even a Social Democratic party must
put maximizing its electorate ahead of maximizing its membership.

SOCIAL STRUCTURE OF ELECTORATE
AND MEMBERSHIP

Social Democratic parties were worker's parties. This title was reflected in party structure by a particularly high percentage of workers among party members and voters. The great majority among the European working classes found a political home in Social Democracy wherever they were struggling for the right to vote during the course of parliamentarization and democratization.

The identification of labor movement and Social Democracy and of the political activity of workers and the Social Democratic party organization became increasingly relative through the decades. Competition from denominational, especially Catholic worker's organizations, drew a sizable minority of the labor movement away from Social Democracy in many countries. Even today in countries with a firm tradition of a Catholic labor movement (Belgium, the Netherlands, in part France and the Federal Republic of Germany as well) the number of workers voting Social Democratic is relatively small, while the percentage of workers voting Christian Democratic (or even Conservative) is relatively high.

Competition from Communist parties from around 1920 successfully challenged Social Democracy for a portion of workers voting for and belonging to Social Democracy in many countries. Today wherever there are strong Communist parties, the number of workers voting for and organized in Social Democratic parties is relatively small, while the proportion of Communist-oriented workers is relatively high.

Overall social development advanced, not least as a result of the effectiveness of Social Democracy and the integration of the workers into society. At the same time the social, economic, and sociopsychological differences between proletarian and bourgeois were being worn away. In conjunction with a steady growth of white-collar workers and an equally discernible decline of blue-collar workers, the focal point of Social Democracy's supporters shifted; if Social Democracy wanted to be successful, it had to have a growing number of white-collar workers and civil servants among its voters and members.

Originally, Social Democratic parties were weighted toward an unequivocally areligious stance. Despite very different positions toward the various religious communities—from the always very open British Labour party to the many emphatically antichurch parties on the Continent—the general attitude of Social Democracy toward religion was rather one of distance, secular and in opposition to the interweaving of church and state. Combined with a general distancing of the worker's movement from the established churches, this led to a pronounced underrepresentation of religiously conscious and active voters and members in the Social Democratic parties.

This contradiction between religion and social democracy, which often became direct antagonism (for example in Spain and Austria during the period between the world wars) and was reflected in party structures, also became more relative over the decades. The position of the churches with regard to the state has changed as much as the corresponding position of social democracy. Today the churches are less inclined than they were at the beginning of this century to enter into alliances with the government and the ruling class or party in the government. Social Democracy is less a party of principled opposition today than at the beginning of the century; more than ever it represents a force that is implicated in the state and that aims to carry out social policy through the state.[14]

In spite of this smoothing out of even the religiously motivated contradiction, the electorate and membership structure of most Social Democratic parties is still characterized by the fact that citizens active in the churches are underrepresented in the individual parties of the Socialist International. The structural tension has outlived the ideological. The social distance is more tenaciously persistent than the programmatic distance.

Another structural feature of all Social Democratic parties has become more relative, though without disappearing altogether: the ambivalent position of women in the Social Democratic parties. The parties basically were among the pioneers in the struggle for women's suffrage, yet essentially they were just as much male-dominated parties. They were male dominated in the sense that at all levels of the party men were in a majority, women in a sometimes nearly nonexistent minority. They were also male dominated in the sense that despite the theoretical receptivity of Social Democracy for the political rights of women, women as voters tended to support Conservative or Christian Democratic parties in disproportionate numbers.[15] Nor has this structural problem area been resolved. To be sure, Social Democratic parties are more open toward women than are bourgeois parties; yet, Social Democratic parties remain male-dominated parties in this dual sense.

Socioeconomic Structures

The central feature of socioeconomic stratification of the electorate of Social Democratic parties is the still dominant but generally decreasing proportion of workers, as well as the also generally increasing numbers of white-collar workers and civil servants. The central feature of socioeconomic stratification of the membership of Social Democratic parties is the low degree of organization of the blue-collar workers and the high degree of organization of the white-collar workers (compared to the composition of the electorate).

The Social Democratic parties remain first and foremost organizations of workers, those dependent on wages. But at the level of voters they are increasingly becoming white-collar parties, while at the membership level this process, expressed in the underrepresentation of the blue collar and the over-representation of the white collar, is ahead of the voter trend.

The trend is unambiguous: Social Democratic parties are going from workers parties to parties of employees. The single case of movement in the other direction (France) is to be attributed to the reformation and renewed rise of the Socialist party of France.

Social democracy is thus adapting to the general development of society; it is adapting its structure to economically and psychologically generated transitions, of which the imprecise, overlapping concept of the white-collar worker is representative. However, social democracy is in no way uniformly represented within this approximately defined group of white-collar workers, which is distinguished by an objective dependence on wages and, at times a subjective distance from the traditional worker's movement. At the lower levels of white-collar workers and civil servants, Social Democratic voters are overrepresented, while at the upper levels they are underrepresented.

Such a distinct stratification is not discernible within the group of blue-collar workers. Skilled workers, who normally are paid better and accorded a higher social status, vote Social Democratic to roughly the same extent as unskilled or semiskilled workers.

The inadequacy of concepts such as blue-collar workers and white-collar workers for explaining voting behavior and thus for explaining the strength or weakness of Social Democratic parties is shown by the importance of sociopsychological determining factors, which have yet to be discussed. However, sociopsychological factors do have to be considered as an explanation for the shift in social representativeness between the

TABLE 9: Examples for Changes in the Social Democratic
Electorate from Blue Collar to White Collar[16]

Social Democratic and Socialist Parties	Socioeconomic Composition of the Electorate in Year					
	1			2		
	A	B	C	A	B	C
Germany (1:1967; 2:1976)	61	32	8	45	49	6
Denmark (1:1971; 2:1975)	61	25	4	64	35	3
Finland (1:1966; 2:1975)	74		26	66	26	8
France (1:1965; 2:1973)	43	25	32	46	24	20
Italy (PSI - 1:1958; 2:1970)	76		24	51		49
Italy (PSDI - 1:1958; 2:1976)	41		59	39		61
Austria (1:1969; 2:1975)	68	25	7	58	35	7

Note: A is the percentage of blue-collar workers; B is the
percentage of white-collar civil servants and employees; C is
the percentage of employers, including peasants.

Sources: For year 1, see Table 3; for year 2, see Joachim
Raschke, ed., Die politischen Parteien in Westeuropa: Geschichte,
Programm, Praxis. Ein Handbuch. Reinbeck, 1978; and William
E. Paterson and Alastair H. Thomas, ed., Social Democratic
Parties in Western Europe. London, 1977.

TABLE 10: Stratification Inside the White Collar (in percent)[17]

	Denmark (1975)		Germany (1976)		France (1973)	
	Electorate	Voters	Electorate	Voters	Electorate	Voters
Civil servants and employees (upper level)	14	9	11	9	9	5
Other civil servants and employees	23	26	35	38	17	22

46

TABLE 11: Stratification Inside the Working Class (in percent)[18]

	Denmark (1975)		Germany (1976)	
	Electorate	Voters	Electorate	Voters
Unskilled and semiskilled workers	20	36	12	15
Skilled workers	16	28	23	28

level of electorate and that of membership. When a collective membership mediated by trade unions is lacking, the membership structure of Social Democratic parties is characterized by a preponderance of white-collar workers. While at the voter level blue-collar workers are still the strongest group, at the membership level they are frequently surpassed by white-collar workers and civil servants.

These assertions are not true for parties whose members are organized for the most part collectively via unions (the British Labour party and the Social Democratic party of Sweden). Yet, how much this shift can alter the social profile of a party is illustrated by the example of the SPD. Within 25 years the number of workers sank to roughly one-quarter, white-collar workers and civil servants became the largest group, and the proportion of students rose from practically nothing to 7 percent.

These differences between electorate and membership are a first indication of the problem of an oligarchy, with which

TABLE 12: Socioeconomic Stratification of Austrian, French, and German Social Democratic and Socialist Parties[19]

Social Democratic and Socialist Parties	Socioeconomic Stratification (in percent)					
	Voters			Members		
	1	2	3	1	2	3
Austria (1969, 1961)	68	25	7	59	35	6
France (1965, 1969)	43	25	32	23		77
Germany (1967, 1968)	61	32	8	49	44	7

Note: 1 is blue-collar workers; 2 is white-collar civil servants and employees; 3 is employers, including peasants. See Table 3 for methodological details.

TABLE 13: Changes in the German Social Democratic Party
(SPD) Membership[20]

	Percent of Total SPD Membership		
	1952	1966	1977
Workers	45	32	28
Employees	17	19	24
Civil servants	5	8	10
Employers	12	5	5
Farmers	2	0	0
Retired	12	18	10
Housewives	7	16	11
Educators	0	1	9+

+7 percent in schools and universities.

Social Democratic parties are confronted just as much as bourgeois or Communist parties. A party is like a pyramid; the
higher the level, the greater the social distortion, and the less
the composition of this level resembles the composition of the
base, and the less Social Democratic organs are characterized
by a proletarian structure.

Workers in Social Democratic parties (and not only in these)
are as much affected by the law of diminishing representation
as are women or voters without a higher education. Their
numbers decline with every subsequent step up the party hierarchy. This law of diminishing representation applies directly
at the first step (the level of members), and it applies to workers
in the parties that appeared in history as worker's parties.

Sociopsychological Structures

Whether a voter votes for a Social Democratic party or
whether a voter joins a Social Democratic party is to be seen
also (but not only) in connection with economic factors. The
reality of Social Democratic electorates and memberships is
shaped by numerous complicated factors, often different from
one nation to the next. In any event, the economic factors
are always accompanied by psychological factors, which can be
observed in every country and for every Social Democratic
party in at least four areas: religion, sex, education, and
social background.

Social democracy's access to the churches and to religious outlooks was as much determined by the power relations of the individual religious communities as by Karl Marx's critique of religion. Although numerous manifestations of the churches' power relations have been overtaken by historical development, and although the philosophical position of Marxism is not regarded in any party of the Socialist International as obligatory or authoritative, still the social distance between social democracy and the churches has remained. Regardless of the ideological or programmatic reconciliation, the social estrangement between the Christian churches, which shape the religious consciousness of Europe, and social democracy has left behind such vestiges. They can be observed especially with the voters and members of the individual Social Democratic parties. The extent of this distance, however, is different from one country to another for historical and national reasons.

One example of a strained relationship that has yet to be entirely resolved programmatically is that between Social Democracy and the church in Italy. The interrelations between clergy and Democrazia Cristiana as well as concrete problem areas (such as the concordat, abortion, divorce, and other contro-

TABLE 14: Correlation Between Religious Behavior and Social Democracy in Italy, 1968[21]

	Party Preference of Working Class (in percent)	
	Regular Church Attendance	Nonregular Church Attendance
Democrazia Cristiana	63	24
PCI (Communists)	5	24
PSI-PSDI	9	20
Other parties	3	7
No answers	20	25
	Party Preference of Middle Class (in percent)	
	Regular Church Attendance	Nonregular Church Attendance
Democrazia Cristiana	56	29
PCI (Communists)	0	7
PSI-PSDI	8	23
Other parties	12	14
No answers	24	27

TABLE 15: Correlation Between Religious Behavior and Social Democracy in Austria (in percent)[22]

Sympathizers of Social Democratic Parties	SPÖ	OeVP[+]	FPOe[+]	Undecided, Others
Church attendance				
Several times per month	16	57	16	27
Once every month	7	10	5	10
Several times per year	32	21	31	23
Almost never	44	12	48	36
No answers	–	–	–	4

Members of Social Democratic Parties	SPÖ	OeVP[+]
Church attendance		
Regular	6	63
At least sometimes	17	23
Almost never, no answer	77	14

[+]OeVP are the Christian Democrats and Conservatives; FPOe are the Right Liberals.

versial issues) account for a distinct distance between Italy's Social Democratic parties and the Catholic Church.

Yet, even in countries in which the historical disputes have essentially been talked out theoretically and in which the church has no direct or indirect alliance with any political party of the center right (such as in Austria), the historical ballast and difference in milieu do influence the relationship between church and Social Democracy at the level of voters. The Social Democratic core milieu and the clerical core milieu are too far removed from one another; the former is traditionally proletarian, the latter is peasant-bourgeois.

This distance, expressed in a marked tendency for church-affiliated voters to vote for parties to the right of Social Democracy and an equally marked inclination on the part of voters without church affiliation to vote Social Democratic, is mainly characteristic of the predominantly Catholic countries of Europe. In countries with Protestant or mixed denominational traditions, the initial situation is a different one. Nevertheless, as in the case of the United Kingdom and the Netherlands, the denominational factor does influence voting behavior and, thus, the structure of the Social Democratic base. In the United Kingdom this is expressed in a distancing of Social Democracy and its voters from the church, which in the past was in league with

TABLE 16: Correlation Between Religious Membership and
Social Democracy in the United Kingdom and the
Netherlands[23]

Party Preference of Church Members	Conserva- tives	Labour	Others
Upper-middle class			
Church of England	75	18	6
Church of Scotland	73	18	9
Nonconformist	59	33	8
Roman Catholic	69	26	5
Others, no membership	55	34	12
Lower-middle class			
Church of England	59	33	8
Church of Scotland	52	35	12
Nonconformist	49	39	11
Roman Catholic	44	48	9
Others, no membership	41	44	15
Working class			
Church of England	41	50	9
Church of Scotland	35	54	12
Nonconformist	39	48	13
Roman Catholic	30	62	8
Others, no membership	32	51	17

Party Preference of Church Members	KVP[+]	ARP[+]	CHU[+]	PvdA	Others
1956					
Roman Catholic	90	1	0	5	4
Dutch Reformist	0	10	29	41	20
Orthodox Reformist	0	85	3	6	6
No membership	1	1	1	72	26
Others	8	5	5	69	13
1968					
Roman Catholic	68	0	0	7	25
Dutch Reformist	1	9	31	36	24
Orthodox Reformist	0	73	2	8	18
No membership	2	1	2	55	40
Others	0	6	6	56	31

[+]KVP is the Catholic People's party; ARP is the Anti-
revolutionary party; CHU is the Christian Historical Union.

the throne and the ruling class. In the Netherlands the religious factor comes into play when individual churches are allied each with a particular party, while Social Democracy represents as a majority the lay milieu remote from but certainly not hostile to the church.

The least important connection between church and religion, on the one hand, and Social Democracy, on the other, appears in homogenously Protestant countries. In the Scandinavian countries, where the relations between church and state and problems of political influence exerted by the church or on the church are simply ancient history, Social Democracy's electorate structure is approximately the same as that of the whole population in the area of religious denominations. The distance between social democracy and religion has been virtually transcended, granted in countries in which the church and religion have become a marginal phenomenon and where they have been reduced to a kindly tolerated concern of a minority.

The denominational factor still influences social democracy today, because social democracy's relation to the Christian churches was in many ways strained in the past. The sex factor does influence today's social democracy, although the Social Democratic parties were always pioneers in the struggle for equality between men and women. Yet, here again there is a gaping contradiction between theory and practice. It was always the left-wing parties that put through women's suffrage in Europe, and it was the women voters who preferred parties of the center right in disproportionate numbers. Left-wing parties, including the Social Democratic parties, were set back by their own success precisely because of women's suffrage.

In the party landscape of Europe today one can still observe this tendency of women voters to vote for moderate right-wing parties in disproportionate numbers over moderate (Social Democratic) and radical (Communist) left-wing parties; but

TABLE 17: Correlation Between Religious Behavior and Social Democracy in Sweden[24]

Church Attendance	Percent of SAP Sympathizers	Percent of Total Electorate
At least once per month	7	15
Several times per year	28	29
Rather seldom	48	41
Never	17	15

TABLE 18: Relation Between Males and Females in the Social Democratic Electorate (in percent)[26]

	Female	Male
France (1973-PS)	47	53
Italy (1968-PSI/PSDI)	33	67
Netherlands (1968-PvdA)	48	52
Sweden (1968-SAP)	48	52

they also prefer them over radical right-wing parties. The Social Democratic parties basically receive disproportionate voter support from men.[25]

The comparatively unfavorable echo that Social Democracy has found among women voters is, however, in the process of changing. There are numerous examples of a tendency toward balance within the Social Democratic electorate. In recent years various Social Democratic parties have suffered exceptionally large losses among men and made exceptionally strong gains among women. All indicators suggest that the paradoxical,

TABLE 19: Examples for Changing Relations Between Men and Women[27]

Party Preference among Male and Female Voters in the United Kingdom (in percent)

	Women		Men	
	October 1974	May 1979	October 1974	May 1979
Labour	38	38	43	38
Conservatives	39	45	32	46
Liberals	20	14	18	13
Others	3	3	7	3

In October 1974, voting behavior was distinctly different between men and women, with a traditional bias of women in favor of the Conservatives; in May 1979, there was no significant difference anymore between female and male voters.

Relation between female and male voters in Austria

	SPÖ		OeVP+	
	Female	Male	Female	Male
March 1973	49	51	56	44
September 1975	54	46	54	46

+OeVP: Christian Democrats and Conservatives.

TABLE 20: Relation of Education to Party Vote in Sweden, 1968[29]

Social Democratic Voters	SAP Voters (in percent)
Primary education in grade school (less than 9 years)	
No further school	63
Vocational school for industrial work	74
Other secondary education (but not gymnasium)	48
Extended primary education and/or at most two years of general secondary education	
At most two years of completing schooling on secondary-education level	39
More than two years of completing secondary education and/or nonuniversity education beyond the secondary level	33
Completed secondary education in gymnasium	
At most two years of education after gymnasium	24
Academic and comparable education	18

historically unjustified distance between women and social democracy is in the process of disappearing.

However, this balancing is to be expected only at the voter level. At the membership level the distance remains very pronounced: women remain a distinct minority. The law of diminishing representation is in full effect: the percentage of women in the membership of Social Democratic parties is everywhere below the percentage of women among the parties' voters. In the membership there are no tendencies in the direction of a shift of the relation between men and women members in favor of women.[28]

Bound up in the socioeconomic factor of profession are not only the socioeconomic factors of income and property indirectly but also the sociopsychological factor of education. Workers earn on average less than nonworkers. Thus, it is only logical that within the electorate of Social Democratic parties voters who have graduated from a secondary school or attained an academic degree are underrepresented, while voters completing only the lower levels are overrepresented.

The sociopsychological factor of education is of great importance for Social Democratic parties inasmuch as it is also

subject to the law of diminishing representation. The group
of voters with below average levels of education becomes increasingly smaller the higher one goes in the datum plane of
the party hierarchy; that is already true for the membership.
For example, the trend in the SPD toward a markedly disproportionate representation of university students shows how much
academics are increasingly being organized in Social Democratic
parties and how strongly the inner life of Social Democratic
parties is being subjected to an academization. Ascending the
pyramid of one of today's Social Democratic parties, the degree
of proletarianization vanishes with the same speed with which
the degree of academization emerges.

That the majority of workers in Europe still vote for Social
Democratic parties—at least the parties that have a government
socialist emphasis—is the one reality. That many workers do
not vote Social Democratic, however, is the other complementary
reality. Besides the Communist parties, which in Italy, France,
Finland, Portugal, and Spain have attracted significant numbers
of working-class voters, the denominational factor has to be
taken into account here, too. Particular church traditions,
especially Catholic and above all in Belgium and the Netherlands,
influence significant portions of the workers in favor of Christian
Democratic parties.

However, the phenomenon of millions of European workers
voting Christian Democratic or Conservative is also a consequence
of the sociopsychological factors of tradition and social origins.
Mattei Dogan has illustrated with the examples of Italy and
France how much a geographic environmental tradition can produce a conservative laborism and how much region and place of
residence can produce conservative voting on the part of
workers. 30

The importance of social background also enters into this
context. In a relatively permeable, mobile society of employees,
it is not enough to draw in the socioeconomic factor "worker"
to explain voting behavior. This factor has to be supplemented
in all cases with the factor "social background." Social Democratic parties are in every case far more preferred by workers
who themselves stem from working-class families than by workers
who come from a bourgeois milieu. Social ascent or social descent
makes the formative power of the in itself unambiguous, socioeconomic determination relative. An executive whose father was
a worker will more likely vote Social Democratic than an executive
with an upper-class background; by the same token, a worker
who comes from a bourgeois family is more likely to vote Conservative or Christian Democratic than a worker born into the
working-class milieu.

TABLE 21: Relation Between Social Origin and Voting Behavior in the United Kingdom[31]

Working-class Voters (in percent)

Party Preference	Below-average Income				Above-average Income			
	Below Age 44		Above Age 44		Below Age 44		Above Age 44	
	Elite Origin	Working-class Origin	Elite Origin	Working-class Origin	Elite Origin	Working-class Origin	Elite Origin	Working-class Origin
Labour	70	86	36	76	64	75	48	81
Conservative	30	14	64	24	36	25	52	19

In spite of clear national differences, the social structure of European Social Democracy reveals a uniform basic pattern. At the voter level, this basic pattern is characterized by the following factors:

Profession: predominance of workers, yet growing tendency in the direction of white-collar workers and civil servants

Religion: detachment, secularized tolerance or indifference, rather opposition or free-church stance than high-church position

Sex: preponderance of men, though general tendency toward establishing a balance between the sexes

Education: graduates of higher education underrepresented, those completing lower levels of schooling overrepresented

Background: lower-class milieu above average, upper-class milieu below average

In some respects this basic pattern of social structure changes considerably at the next level, that of membership.

Profession: workers subject to the law of diminishing representation, at least the directly structured parties are already white-collar parties at the membership level

Sex: women subject to the law of diminishing representation, at the membership level, European Social Democracy is determined by men

Education: those finishing only the lower levels of schooling subject to the law of diminishing representation, at the membership level there is a distinct trend toward academization

Social structure points to a fundamental dilemma of social democracy: in order to be successful in the given social order and in order to be able to change the given social order, social democracy must adapt itself to the prevailing order in essential points. It performs this adaptation in its social structure as well.

PARTY FINANCING

From the start the Social Democratic parties as mass and membership parties have been distinguished from their rival bourgeois parties by a fundamentally different financial base. Social Democracy came out against the existing social relations; it set itself in opposition to the ruling interests and thus the interests of the ruling classes. It could, therefore, not count on being supported financially by those ruling interests, as were the Liberals and Conservatives. Its objective of gaining the broadest possible membership base was designed to create the necessary preconditions for an alternative financing through the members themselves.[32]

This initial situation has, of course, shifted, but in its essential features it is true of today's social democracy as well. The finances of the Social Democratic parties exhibit some common characteristics. On the income side this means a comparatively great importance of income from membership dues, comparatively little importance of income from donations, and some substantial financial allocations from the trade unions, especially in the case of Social Democratic parties with indirect structure.

Social democracy as a prototype of a mass membership party also has taken an organizational form that has had considerable impact on the expenditure side. The professionalization and vertical organization of the party apparatus was always cost-intensive; in contrast, the outlays incurred directly for election campaigns were relatively small. Basically this differentiation on the expenditure side can be observed with the Social Democratic parties of the present: they have relatively heavy outlays for the ongoing party work, independent of general elections, and relatively little expenditure for the campaigns themselves.

These characteristics (common to all Social Democratic parties) are being increasingly refined by the growing importance of state financing for political parties, which by its very nature diminishes the differences between the individual parties, and by the general pull toward convergence, which Social Democratic parties see themselves exposed to and which influences their financing. Nevertheless, all available empirical evidence shows that Social Democratic parties still exhibit certain characteristic features in financing. Although party financing is that area of the party landscape most withdrawn from the public and from political science research, the feasible analyses confirm the general assertions.

Characteristics of Social Democratic
Party Financing

The traditional sources of income for political parties are donations and membership dues. Donations are of prime importance for parties with a low degree of organization and for parties

TABLE 22: Union and Party Financing of Social Democracy
in the United Kingdom, 1967-72[33]

Source	Percent of Income
Unions	57
Membership dues	29
Cooperatives	10
Donations	1
Property	3

with an upper-class social base. Membership dues are of importance primarily for parties with a high degree of organization
and a lower-class social base.

For some Social Democratic parties these traditional sources
are supplemented considerably by the funds that come from the
unions. The prime example of this is the British Labour party.
For British Social Democrats the membership dues, which
originally were decisive for Continental Social Democrats, are
of secondary importance. Collective membership via the unions
also shapes the party's financial situation.

For the majority of Social Democratic parties, which are
characterized not by an indirect but solely by a direct structure,
the possibility for financing by and via the unions is not applicable. However, in many countries the Social Democrats, in line
with other parties, have tapped an increasingly important source
of financing: the state. According to definite distribution ratios,
the state gives individual parties public monies, thus recognizing
the central importance of the parties for modern democracy.
Supplementary to this, another indirect form of state financing
of parties has taken root precisely in the case of Social Democratic parties: the internal party taxation of politicians, who
have their party to thank for their mandates or other positions.
State financing and party assessments have become an important
possibility for the financing of many Social Democratic parties.

TABLE 23: Income of a Social Democratic Party in a System
of Party Financing by the State—Austria, 1976[34]

Source	Percent of Income
Membership dues	53
Internal taxation	14
Donations	2
State (direct by law)	10
State (indirect)	20

TABLE 24: Income of a Social Democratic Party
in a System of Party Financing by the
State—Portugal, 1976-77[35]

Source	Percent of Income
Membership dues	22
Internal taxation	9
State	59
Sale of party publications	9

State financing is becoming the decisive source of income,
especially for parties that show a weak degree of organization
and have no backing from financially strong circles of donors.
A prime example of this is the Socialist party of Portugal. For
this party of modest organizational strength and only modest
backing from donations, the monies distributed by the state
have become far and away its most important financial security.

The increasing dependence of Social Democracy on state
financing offers the parties great advantages. State financing
of parties subjects to certain public control that realm of modern
parties that can especially escape control and be particularly
menaced by criminal activity. State financing of parties means
that the appropriation of funds must be fully public; certain
information has to be given concerning the magnitude of financing.
State financing of parties in addition offers Social Democratic
parties the particular advantage that the relative financial
margin of the large established parties of the center right (Conservatives, Christian Democrats, and Liberals) is diminished,
since state financing can be oriented exclusively to the size of
the parties and thereby has a leveling effect on the right-left
spectrum. State financing of parties means that Social Democracy
makes up financial ground on its bourgeois rivals.

State financing of parties does, however, entail certain
disadvantages, too. The state that gives the parties funds is
an instrument of these parties itself. The members of parliament
who pass the laws on the remittance of public monies to the
parties and who manipulate the state's money tap are party
officials. State financing of parties also means that the parties
can help themselves directly to the state coffers. This aspect
at least partly reverses the positive control aspect. In general,
the parties can improve their financial situations without having
to produce any additional legitimation. For a party that claims
to change the state and society gradually but substantially,
this form of self-service financing brings an additional temptation

to compromise and to integrate into existing relations. In any event, this trend in party financing induces Social Democracy more than ever to accommodate.

However, in the consciousness of Social Democracy the positive aspect tends to be predominant. A comparative sampling has revealed that in Social Democratic-dominated Norway those sympathetic to Social Democracy had a more positive attitude toward state financing of parties than the sympathizers of parties to the right of center. The fact that a similar attitude can be discerned among voters of the Democratic party in the United States can be explained by a parallel social structure; the Democratic party is also disproportionately based on the weaker strata of society and is akin to European Social Democracy.

The lines of development for income structure reinforce the general trend toward accommodation among the large parties of Europe. Still the convergence in financing has in no way advanced to the point of identity. Between Social Democratic and bourgeois parties there remain as always significant differences both in income structures and in expenditure structures. State financing of parties does make these differences more relative; however, membership dues remain of crucial importance for Social Democratic parties, as do donations for bourgeois parties.

A comparison of the incomes of the two large party groupings in the Federal Republic of Germany demonstrates not only the differences that continue to shape the parties' income struc-

TABLE 25: Public Opinion about Party Financing by the State in the United States and Norway[36]

Question: "Would you like or dislike if the government financed some parts of the campaign costs of parties or candidates?"

| | Answers (in percent) | | |
	Like	Dislike	Don't Know or No Answer
United States (1964)			
Total electorate	11	71	18
Democrats	12	71	17
Republicans	9	82	9
Norway (1964)			
Total electorate	20	48	32
Socialists	23	44	32
Nonsocialists	18	54	28

TABLE 26: Income of Social Democrats and Nonsocialists in the German SPD and CDU/CSU[37]

| | Income in absolute figures (in 1000 DM) | | | | | |
| | SPD | | CDU | | CSU | |
Source	1976	1977	1976	1977	1976	1977
Membership dues	55,493	56,391	37,952	43,043	4,544	5,531
Internal taxation	10,802	11,796	10,774	11,869	1,930	2,120
Property	1,701	1,167	2,033	2,434	208	191
Activities and publications	1,312	299	2,199	1,360	612	450
Donations	19,583	6,167	53,744	24,867	12,599	6,715
Credits	15,176	13,103	9,903	3,480	4,852	3,707
State	30,787	14,136	36,207	13,416	9,035	4,060
Other	3,787	3,167	1,597	722	*	256
Total	138,641	106,226	154,409	101,191	33,780	23,030

*Statistics not applicable.

tures; it also shows how divergent the expenditure structures are. In the election year 1976 the Christlich-Demokratische Union/Christlich-Soziale Union (CDU-CSU) had a much more distinct financial advantage over the SPD than in 1977, a non-election year in which the SPD more or less pulled even. Of course, both parties brought in more in the election year because they had to spend more; however, the additional receipts were much greater for the Union parties than for the Social Democrats. Accordingly, the Union parties were able to invest much more money directly in the election campaign than the Social Democrats. The traditional difference in the structure of expenditures is once again evident. Parties to the right of center spend relatively more in the election campaign, and relatively less for party work unrelated to campaigning; Social Democratic parties spend relatively more for the permanent work and relatively less for the election campaign in the stricter sense. In an election, bourgeois parties can much more effectively mobilize additional financial resources, because they can much more effectively speak to the interests behind such financial strength. Despite their integration and established position, Social Democratic parties are not the prime representatives of the dominant social and financial interests.

The financing of a political party is always indicative of the party's position in society. The financing of today's Social Democratic parties affords substantial indication of the process of change in social democracy from the type of party that over the decades had to solicit regular payments of modest membership dues from the socially weaker classes to a type of party that knows how to draw upon the whole range of financing possibilities. The European Social Democracy of the present is no longer the poor outsiders' party, standing at the head of the outcasts of society. European Social Democracy is a powerful party, which is near the centers of power or has already occupied these centers.

Still, Social Democracy is also, precisely because of its financial basis, in no way a party like any other. Nowhere has it become the party of big money or big business. Nowhere are Social Democratic parties financed to any great extent by industry and industry federations; these groupings everywhere prefer the rival bourgeois parties. In the course of its history, Social Democracy has certainly been able to establish itself; nowhere does it appear as a poor party. But neither has it become the instrument of social interests against which it has contended. The dialectical tension in which modern Social Democracy exists also dominates its financial situation.

Social Democracy and the Media

The organization of Social Democratic mass parties originally included a Social Democratic press organization, which was designed to set up against bourgeois public opinion a Social Democratic counteropinion. The bourgeois parties of notables could rely on fundamental sympathy in the prevailing organs of the press, even if the newspapers of the late nineteenth and early twentieth centuries were without exception independent (in the sense of not being bound to a particular party). Social democracy criticized this notion of independence and counterposed conscious partiality against the unconscious partiality of the dominant bourgeois press.

As long as Social Democratic parties were getting stronger from a position of principled opposition, the Social Democratic press empire grew as well. However, as soon as Social Democratic parties started becoming more and more a part of prevailing relations, the Social Democratic press progressively came to a crisis. Because the supporters of the now established, large Social Democratic parties no longer had to feel like society's

outsiders, they no longer had the old need for a Social Democratic counterculture, a contrary Social Democratic public opinion,
or a Social Democratic inner solidarity in the face of a disapprov-
ing bourgeois environment. The rise of social democracy fostered
the absorbing of the Social Democratic subculture into a dominant
culture changed by it, and it fostered the dying out of the
Social Democratic press.

This process of atrophy of the traditional Social Democratic
press must, of course, also be seen in conjunction with general
conditions of concentration. Technological developments led to
a fundamental reduction in the number of newspapers in all the
nations of Europe, while total circulation was growing. These
developments especially resulted in party newspapers getting
caught in an economic-technological bind, which gradually
destroyed their livelihood.

However, this process of atrophy of the traditional Social
Democratic press does not apply to all parties to the same extent.
Successful Social Democratic parties in the smaller European
countries (Sweden, Austria, the Netherlands, and Belgium)
have been hit by this process to a lesser extent than successful
Social Democratic parties in the larger countries (the United
Kingdom and the Federal Republic of Germany). Those less
successful parties of the opposition socialist type have been
affected to a lesser extent. Where, despite political success,
a Social Democratic subculture or camp mentality continues to
exist (Austria, the Netherlands, and Sweden) or where, lacking
such success, the subculture exists (Italy), the parties continue
to make use of their own daily newspapers. Of course, the
Italian Avanti or the Austrian Arbeiter-Zeitung also have to
contend with growing financial difficulties, but they have managed
to survive all the crises up to now.

It is remarkable that the two Social Democratic parties
that are able to mobilize the most supporters—in absolute figures—
no longer control their own daily newspapers. The British
Labour party and the Social Democratic party of Germany have
in many ways converted their traditional daily newspapers;
these two parties are no longer represented in their countries'
central market for daily newspapers, at least not directly from
the party's own organ. The history of the dying out or the
changing of newspapers so rich in tradition as the Daily Herald
and Vorwärts shows the ambivalence of the Social Democratic
rise; in some sectors the rise can go hand in hand with a decline.

The Daily Herald, endowed with trade union funds, was
one of the great dailies of the United Kingdom during the interwar period. For a time its circulation reached over 1.5 million.

After the Second World War, as the Labour party finally established itself as a counterpart to the Conservatives in the British two-party system and repeatedly took over and lost again the reins of government in typical British swings of the political pendulum, the party and unions could no longer maintain the Daily Herald. In the place of a daily newspaper bound to party and union there came the system of a newspaper associated with the Labour party, represented by the Sun. The Labour party turned to persuading particular papers from among the non-party-bound press to write from an essentially sympathetic standpoint. Thus the Labour party, which can regularly win more than 10 million voters, is left without its own paper in competition with British newspapers, though it is supported by a basic current of sympathy by a few newspapers, such as the Sun and the Daily Mirror.[38]

The second Social Democratic party that can always count on reaching more than 10 million voters, the SPD, is in a similar situation. After the rule of National Socialism had completely destroyed the Social Democratic press and publishing system, the SPD did not find the way back to its old press power after 1945. Various attempts at surviving at least regionally with daily papers bound directly to the party came to nothing. The Vorwärts, since 1876 the official organ of German Social Democracy, appears only as an official party weekly with modest circulation. Despite its organizational strength, even the SPD is without its own daily newspaper on the central press market of the Federal Republic of Germany.[39]

The Social Democrats were able to bear this decline of the party press relatively easily, because the significance of the print media was supplemented and made relative by the significance of the electronic media. After 1945 the media policy of Social Democracy has increasingly devoted critical attention to radio and television. Social Democratic media policy today is less press policy and more radio and television policy.

Since the electronic media in Europe are in general organized according to the principle of national broadcasting corporations (in part supplemented by private corporations, such as the supplementing of the British Broadcasting Corporation by the private Independent Télévision (ITV), Social Democratic media policy is also aimed at capturing positions of control in the realm of government influence over radio and television. Hence, social democracy is primarily intent on gaining influence according to individual party strengths.

This tendency toward proportionality thinking in media policy roughly characterizes the stance of the German, Austrian, and Italian Social Democrats and Socialists. It also characterizes the critical position of the French Socialists, who reproach the state-run Office de Radiodiffusion-Television Francaise (ORTF) with inadequate balance, that is with a lack of political proportion and a preponderance of right-wing (Liberal, Conservative, and Gaullist) tendencies.

The situation in the Netherlands diverges fundamentally from this inclination to use electronic media policy in the active interest of party balance and party proportionality. The system of segmented pluralism, which governs the whole political culture and the political system of the Netherlands, also encompasses the segmentation of the electronic media. Since any social group can apply for and obtain specific broadcast times for radio and television, there has developed alongside denominational broadcasting corporations a radio corporation of a Social Democratic stamp, the Vereiniging van Arbeiters Radioamateurs (VARA). Thus, in the Netherlands the Labor party (PvdA) operates de facto its own Social Democratic radio and television stations. The partially atrophied system of party newspapers exists in the Netherlands as an analogue to radio and television broadcasting based on parties and camps.[40]

Of course, in the Netherlands one can observe a process that has long been at work in the press sector as a consequence of the integration of social democracy and of the individual subcultures (segments or camps) into society, the segmented corporations dependent on a political perspective have been losing ground to the nonsegmented secularized corporations. The approaching end of the Social Democratic subculture, which is discernible everywhere (though at various rates of progress), has not stopped at the Dutch system of Social Democratic radio and television.[41]

At first glance, the development of a Social Democratic media policy seems to be in contradiction to the financial strength of the Social Democratic parties. Social Democracy has managed to supplement substantially its traditional sources of income through new claims to income. State financing of parties in particular as well as financing by trade unions today enables Social Democratic parties to compete on roughly an equal footing with the large parties to the right of center. In the media sector, however, Social Democratic influence is a victim of financial weakness at least to the extent that Social Democratic newspapers fall victim to commercial constraints with increasing frequency.

Yet, this is only an apparent contradiction. The financial strength of Social Democracy today is an expression of the economic strength of a party grouping that has worked out for itself a permanent place in the individual political systems. However, the old forms of Social Democracy's media and especially press policy emanated from a ghetto situation and from a withdrawal into the shell of a specifically Social Democratic subculture. The establishment of European Social Democracy had to entail, even if with some delay, the gradual breakup of the ghetto walls, the segments, and the camps. Along with their party, the supporters of Social Democracy have also been integrated. Their consciousness increasingly demands less specifically Social Democratic information; to a greater and greater extent they feel satisfied by media that are neither expressly Social Democratic nor expressly antisocialist.

The Social Democratic press of the traditional style is on its deathbed. In part it has already reached the end, because Social Democracy has become a permanent power factor in all of Europe.

INTRAPARTY DEMOCRACY

Historically, social democracy has always committed itself not only to democracy in the state but to democracy in the party. Intraparty democracy was a fundamentally undisputed postulate for all Social Democratic parties. The conflicts emerging in the party over issues of policy and leadership were to be resolved according to democratic guidelines.

The basic idea of intraparty democracy was also underscored by the division between the Bolshevik-Communist principle of a cadre party and the Menshevik-Social Democratic principle of a mass party, which first broke out in 1903 and was firmly established after 1917. The decision for the mass and membership party was also a decision against the suspension of intraparty democracy in favor of revolutionary action, a course sanctioned at least indirectly for a time by the Leninist principle of organization.

Robert Michels has already demonstrated that the undisputed principle of internal democracy was not always fully realized in the practice of Social Democratic parties, even at this point of transition from the integral to the pluralistic stage of development. The "iron law of oligarchy" had taken hold, especially in Social Democratic parties. The type of professionally organized mass party especially allowed for an emancipation of the elected from the electors. The history of intraparty democracy in social democracy is the history of the tension between undisputed democratic claims and tendential oligarchic reality.[42]

As a general postulate, intraparty democracy has been concretized in party constitutions in the form of a representative democracy. Intraparty democracy consists in the concentration of formal decision-making authority in the party conference or party congress. The assembly of, in most cases, indirectly selected delegates from the individual party organs is the party parliament. The representatives of the party's individual organizations, groups, and tendencies come together at regular intervals to make basic decisions on party policy and leadership.

The frequency with which the party parliaments (party conferences and party congresses) have to meet varies. The British Labour party, for example, once a year organizes its party conference, which functions as a party parliament. Other parties have allowed longer intervals between party congresses; however, between the regular party conferences special party conferences (extraordinary party congresses) are frequently convened.

Party parliaments differ according to the direct or indirect structure of the overall organization. Social Democratic parties with indirect structure have a concurrence of closed voting blocks of the suborganizations and delegates of the individual members. Social Democratic parties with direct structure know only a delegate system, which in most cases reflects the regional structuring of the whole party and its individual members. Again the British Labour party serves as an example of an indirectly structured party. The block of trade unions controls practically 90 percent of the entire vote potential of a party conference. The block voting of the individual unions thus dominates the whole party parliament.[43] The party conferences of the SPD exemplify a party parliament of an exclusively directly structured party. The party conference is the assembly of delegates who come to the party conference through an indirect process from the approximately 10,000 local party branches, 250 area organizations, 22 regional organizations, and 11 Land associations.[44]

In general, however, party parliaments are not parliaments in the sense of modern, national party parliamentarism. Party conferences and party congresses are often marked by the open settlement of intraparty conflicts; however, faction-like groupings are the exception. The party parliaments of Social Democracy only rarely give full expression to intraparty pluralism. An example of this exception is the Socialist party of France. At its party conference, competing resolutions are voted upon, and any resolution that obtains more than 5 percent of the delegates' votes is represented proportionally in the directorate and

the executive bureau. In this way the French Socialists have
institutionalized intraparty pluralism and have made the party
conference the actual arena for settling conflicts over personali-
ties and issues. [45]

Recruitment of Political Elites

Democratic claim and democratic statutes can alter nothing
in the way labor is divided within Social Democratic parties.
Social Democratic parties must also send representatives into
parliament and government; Social Democratic parties also have
party headquarters and party officials. The way in which the
individual parties decide on filling these elite positions allows
for conclusions as to the actual importance of internal democracy
and to the actual importance of the extent of the parties' integration into society.

In their essential characteristics, the leading officials of
European Social Democracy are different from the rank and file
of their parties. In recruiting their elites, the Social Democratic
parties indirectly and unintentionally carry out a selection process
that emphasizes the social distance between the rank and file
and leadership. There is an emphasis on white-collar workers
over blue-collar workers; the Social Democratic elites in government and party are to a much lesser extent workers by social
background than the voters and members. There is an emphasis
on men over women; the proportion of women among Social Democratic elites is very small. Finally, there is an emphasis on
academic education; the proportion of graduates of higher education is very high among Social Democratic elites.

The differences in the social structure between electors
and elected are in no way stable; they are getting larger. While
the proportion of workers in the Social Democratic electorate
has more or less stabilized, showing only slightly a downward
trend, the number of those who were workers prior to their
parliamentary careers has rapidly declined among the Social
Democratic mandataries. Even in the case of the British Labour
party, where the collective membership via the unions guarantees
a high proportion of working-class members, the number of
workers elected to the House of Commons has decreased rapidly.
Even if the number of Labour mandataries whose established
callings are working-class occupations is still well above the
proportion of analogous Conservative parliamentarians, the
example of Labour members of parliament (MPs) shows the
process of social convergence. The criteria governing the

selection of Social Democratic elites approximate the criteria
that have always been decisive in bourgeois parties.

Social Democratic women are the second group subject to
the law of diminishing representation within the party hierarchy.
The negligible representation of women among the elites is in
no way simply a transitional phenomenon; rather, as can be
seen with the SPD and the British Labour party, the number
of female Social Democratic parliamentarians is even going down
slightly. There is nothing to suggest that the underrepresentation of Social Democratic women in the leadership bodies can be
substantially altered in the hear future. Committed in theory
to the emancipation of women, Social Democracy differs from the
extremely male-dominated bourgeois rival parties only by degree
not fundamentally.

The tendency toward Social Democratic leadership's de-
creasingly representative character in relation to the structural
features of the Social Democratic rank and file is further influenced by the professionalization of politics. A substantial
portion of those belonging to the parliamentary and intraparty
elites consists of full-time party or trade union officials. It is
everywhere evident how a professionalized party apparatus
committed to efficiency leads to the independent position of
party managers; to a great extent it is professional politicians
who are speaking and acting for Social Democratic voters and
members. The party apparatus itself furnishes the functionaries
to direct the party apparatus in the name of the voters and
members. The representatives of the people, particularly the
Social Democratic representatives, are frequently party officials
and trade union officials.

TABLE 27: Percentage of Workers in the Social Democratic
Electorate and Among Social Democratic Representatives in Germany and France[46]

	Workers in the Electorate (in percent)			Workers among Members in Parliament (in percent)		
Germany—SPD (1967, 1969)	61	32	8	0	89	10
France—SFIO (1965, 1968)	43	25	32	0	74	26

Note: For members of parliament, not the former but the
actual profession was considered.

TABLE 28: Social Changes—Labour Members of Parliament—
British House of Commons[47]

Workers Inside the Labour Party (in percent)

1945	27	1964	18
1950	26	1966	16
1951	26	1970	13
1955	25	1974 (Feb.)	12
1959	21	1974 (Oct.)	12

Educational Stratification Inside the Labour Party (in percent)

	1	2	3		1	2	3
1945	43	34	15	1964	30	44	18
1950	41	38	15	1966	26	49	19
1951	39	39	17	1970	22	51	20
1955	38	38	16	1974 (Feb.)	19	53	19
1959	36	40	17	1974 (Oct.)	16	56	21

Note: 1 indicates compulsory schools only; 2 indicates a university education; 3 indicates an education at Oxford or Cambridge.

TABLE 29: Percent of Women in the British House of Commons
and in the German Bundestag[48]

Women in the House of Commons

	C	L	O		C	L	O
1945	0.5	5.3	7.4	1964	3.7	5.6	0.0
1950	2.0	4.4	7.7	1966	2.8	5.2	0.0
1951	1.8	3.7	0.0	1970	4.5	3.4	10.0
1955	2.8	5.1	0.0	1974 (Feb.)	3.0	4.3	2.7
1959	3.3	5.0	0.0	1974 (Oct.)	2.5	5.6	5.1

Note: C = Conservatives; L = Labour party; O = all other parties.

Women in the Bundestag

	C	S	F	O		C	S	F	O
1949	7.8	9.5	1.9	5.0	1965	6.0	8.8	4.0	0.0
1953	7.6	12.9	5.7	4.4	1969	5.6	7.6	6.5	0.0
1957	7.9	12.0	7.0	5.5	1972	6.8	6.6	7.1	0.0
1961	7.2	10.3	6.0	0.0	1976	7.5	6.7	10.0	0.0

Note: C = Christian Democrats; S = SPD; F = Liberals; O = all other parties.

TABLE 30: Position of Full-time Party Officials and Union
Officials in the Swedish Parliament and in Norwegian
Party Leadership[49]

Social Structure of Swedish Reichstag (in percent)

	SAP+ 1945	SAP 1968	Center 1968	Liberals 1968	Conservatives 1968
Higher civil servants and employees, employers	5	24	23	45	42
Lower civil servants and employees, small business-men	17	28	9	35	10
Farmers	23	2	56	8	32
Workers	38	12	—	4	3
Party officials	—	34	12	8	13

+Data for 1945 concerning social origin and not concerning
actual professions (like data for 1968); the comparison between
1945 and 1968 is limited and the sum of all data for 1945 is not
100 because not all data for 1945 could be included in the scheme
of professions.

Social Structure of Party Leadership of Norwegian Labor Party
(in percent)

	0	1	2	3	4	5	6	7	8	9	10	11	N
1887-1903	0	0	2	6	34	0	1	11	24	11	12	0	140
1904-17	9	1	9	24	10	3	3	4	9	4	25	1	106
1918-26	4	6	4	19	4	4	9	6	8	6	28	2	191
1927-39	15	4	4	8	2	8	5	7	3	3	38	4	184
1945-49	23	11	2	8	5	6	4	2	0	0	35	3	97
1950-59	21	19	2	13	3	2	2	1	0	0	38	1	167
1960-65	22	17	5	9	2	0	3	2	0	1	35	5	130
1966-71	12	19	9	3	4	2	0	2	1	2	44	2	129

Note: 0 = members of parliament and of the cabinet; 1 =
higher civil servants; 2 = lower civil servants; 3 = journalists
and editors; 4 = employers and higher employees; 5 = lower
employees; 6 = farmers and fishermen; 7 = industrial workers;
8 = artisans; 9 = workers outside industry; 10 = party and
union officials; 11 = housewives; N = number of all party representatives examined.

The rank-and-file democratic claim of a mass membership party and the immense fact of unrepresentative elites assume a particular form in the structure of Austrian Social Democracy. Over a long period the Austrian Socialist party (SPÖ) has developed the organizational and promotional model of Vertrauensleute. Roughly 10 percent of all party members in this tightly organized party undergo specific training programs and then become, as Vertrauensleute, the base of party officialdom, from which the higher officials are recruited. Roughly 10 percent of the membership thus become cadre, and the model of the mass and membership party is supplemented by the model of the cadre party.[50] However, the relatively broad, uniform official stratum of Vertrauensleute in the SPÖ is as much shaped by the law of diminishing representation as are the elites of this and other Social Democratic parties. Thus, among the members of the SPÖ's far and away largest and most tightly organized Land association, Vienna, the relation of men to women amounts to 54 to 46. Among the Vertrauensleute of the Vienna SPÖ, however, the proportion comes to 67 men to 33 women.[51]

Intraparty Conflicts

Social Democratic parties have known and now know internal contradictions. With the end of the initial stage of integral Marxism and the rise of disputes over revisionism and other conflicts over direction, there began for Social Democracy the problem of having to settle internal conflicts in such a way that neither the postulate of intraparty democracy nor the necessity for efficient unity should come to harm.

In the Social Democracy of today, an ideological and in part organizational factionalism is the rule. With the exception of the Social Democratic parties of Denmark, Austria, and Sweden, intraparty conflicts can be identified in an organized form.[52] Individual groups in the parties have mutually distinguishable positions that contend with one another openly. Organized intraparty conflict in Social Democracy has two dimensions: organizational and ideological.

The ideological dimension can be explained essentially by the right-left spectrum. Social Democratic parties have various wings, behind which there are varying conceptions of strategy and also of goals. With the exception of the three above-mentioned parties, these differences are apprehended and solidified by intraparty organizations.

In the Belgian Socialist party (BSP-PSB) the ideological range of tensions coincides to some extent with Belgium's essentially regional tensions. The Walloon party organization is dominated by a left-wing, principle-oriented direction that stresses the property question; the Flemish regional organization, on the other hand, is controlled by a right-wing, practice-oriented tendency that tends to neglect the property question. The regionalization of party structure in Belgian Social Democracy has further strengthened this coupling of regional and ideological conflicts, since the French and Dutch language groups each elect one of the two presidents of the BSP-PSB.[53]

The British Labour party likewise furnishes an institutional-organizational framework for ideological tensions. The party conference is dominated by the large trade union blocks, which since the mid-1960s have usually inclined toward the left of the ideological spectrum. The counterweight to a rather left-wing party conference is the rather right-wing parliamentary caucus. The Labour MPs in the House of Commons, who are on the whole traditionally inclined to pragmatism (that is, of a more right-wing ideological leaning), constitute an institution serving to make the importance of the party conference and its decisions relative. The role of the caucus is actually exceedingly strong in the United Kingdom: the caucus elects the head of the party and, thus, the prime minister or opposition leader. If the Labour party is in opposition, then the weight of the party conference tends to be greater; if the Labour party is in power, then in general the caucus is accorded increased significance.[54]

The Italian Socialists' (PSI) factionalism has come to approximate the correnti factionalism of the Christian Democrats. In the PSI a personal following becomes an ideological-institutional subparty, and the party as a whole is then ruled by changing coalitions. The party's line becomes relatively unpredictable; the conflicts within the party, however, become relatively transparent.[55]

One particular form of institutionalizing ideological conflicts has developed in the SPD and in the Norwegian Labor party. For quite some time, the SPD's Young Socialists and likewise the Norwegian Labor party's youth organization have developed into organs of intraparty opposition. Both Social Democratic youth groups are instruments of the left wing, which can confront the predominant government socialism of the party leadership with open criticism and alternative conceptions.[56]

Joachim Raschke has studied the conditions for success of an intraparty opposition in Social Democratic parties. Electoral success and successful work in government; close ties with large, cooperative trade unions; and a strong national and political consensus represent poor preconditions for the emergence of intraparty opposition.[57] Since these general conditions are also defining characteristics of government socialism, the intensity and institutionalization of intraparty conflicts can be linked with the dichotomy of government socialism and opposition socialism. The stronger the inclination toward opposition socialism, the greater the probability of a factionalism that leads to the formation of permanent factions and that establishes a kind of multiparty system within Social Democracy. The factionalism in the two typical opposition Socialist parties, the Italian Socialists (PSI) and the French Socialists (PS), documents this: the formation of correnti with the Italians and the legitimation of a multifaction system at the French party conference represent extreme cases of open intraparty rivalry.

In structuring intraparty democracy, Social Democracy is currently confronting the alternative of either promoting social representation at the cost of political efficiency or maximizing political efficiency to the detriment of social representation. Social Democracy is very clearly deciding in favor of efficiency. Thus, it confirms the fundamental correctness of the oligarchy diagnosis; it has clearly submitted to leadership by a social elite. Political specialization has assumed the place of proletarian loyalty.

Social Democratic parties are worker's parties, people's parties, and elite parties simultaneously.[58] They are worker's parties, because in general they are able to mobilize the majority of the workers as voters; they are people's parties, because they are successful in reaching other large groups in society beyond the working class; and they are elite parties, because in the course of intraparty recruiting they give preference indirectly to existing, elitist criteria of efficiency.

Thus, Social Democracy structures the principle of intraparty democracy in a form essentially analogous to the other established parties, in particular bourgeois parties. The elites legitimated by and speaking for the Social Democratic parties are more and more rapidly assuming the academic white-collar profile, which has always distinguished Liberal, Conservative, and Christian Democratic parties. Of course, this says nothing about the substance of Social Democratic politics; but it does give an indication of the strength of the general pull toward convergence.

One measure of the realization of intraparty democracy is the degree of tolerance a party shows toward intraparty opposition. This tolerance is certainly highly developed today among the Social Democratic parties. Of course, it is a tolerance that is principally characteristic of all Americanizing people's parties— the people's and catchall parties of the right as well as those of the left center. Social Democratic parties only rarely resort to the instrument of expulsion from the party. Precisely the large and successful parties, with the emphasis on government socialism, only rarely experience struggles over direction that end up in expulsions or splits.

However, this tolerance is also indifference. Social Democratic elites can afford to be indifferent toward intraparty criticism and intraparty discussion of goals. As soon as they submit fully, with a government socialist orientation, to the legalities of the multiparty system, their deciding standard becomes not a correctness of socialist content but rather the ability to win elections. The representatives of the second and third echelon may dispute on matters of ideology; on the parties' policies it is the first echelon that decides, and their primary goal is winning elections in order to be able to govern.

5
Positions in the Political System

Socialism will come not as the result of a great
political battle of decision, but rather as a consequence of a series of economic and political
victories of the workers movement in the various
areas of its activity; not as a reaction to a heavier
oppression, greater suffering, further humiliation
of the working people, but as a consequence of
their growing social influence and the relative
improvements in the economic, political and general
social (moral) conditions.

Eduard Bernstein[1]

In this sense Eduard Bernstein has prevailed in social
democracy; in this sense the Social Democratic and Socialist
parties in Europe today are thoroughly revisionist. Their politics
are not aimed at creating an ideal society by means of a fundamental social act, called a revolution; their goal is to change
the state and society step by step. Socialism may remain a
splendid vision, which amid the daily toil inspires and fires the
imagination. The practice of socialism, however, is a most
tangible one, which often has scarcely any connection with the
socialist vision.

If social democracy is more than an arbitrary label, more
than a name plate that goes with any and all conceivable political
contents; if social democratic has yet to become an attribute
that can be exchanged with any other concepts to suit the prevailing fashion; if the Social Democratic parties of today stand
for a minimum of characteristic commonality, then this must be

discernible in the surrounding social environment. Social democracy is, at least according to the claim of the parties committed to it, not an end in itself; it is a means to the end of transforming the state and society in the direction of humanity and socialism.

Social Democratic parties must, therefore, furnish proof that the How, but especially the What, of their politics sets them apart. If social democracy can truly build a better society, then wherever Social Democratic parties possess the instruments for political construction, there must be at least some evidence of the better society. Regardless of whether humanity and socialism are concrete, good goals, if the goals that social democracy has set itself are serious ones, then Social Democratic politics and the social democratic shaping of society must be different, particularly from Conservative, Christian Democratic, Liberal, and Communist politics. Even if it can only be a matter of a relative differentiation, in the sense of Eduard Bernstein's concept of socialism, no judgment of history could be as deadly for social democracy as the following conclusion: its political efforts don't have other recognizable, that is distinguishable consequences typical for social democracy.

GOVERNMENT AND OPPOSITION ROLES

Social Democratic parties in Europe are situated in political systems displaying numerous variations on the basic notion of parliamentary government. With the exception of Switzerland, all the states in which the parties examined here operate are parliamentary systems.[2] This means that the government is politically responsible to the parliament; that the parliamentary majority and government are, therefore, as a rule politically coordinated; and that the institutional separation of powers (legislative and executive) has made way for the temporal separation of powers (government and opposition).[3]

By their very nature, Social Democratic parties are forces of action and not, say, of sheer protest; they tend toward action and not toward standing on the sidelines. Their claim to want to and to be able to change society—even if only gradually—forces them into the proximity of political power. Abstinence from power would exclude changes; reforms presuppose power.

The essence of Social Democratic parties also includes full acceptance of the groundrules of party pluralism. Social Democracy has indeed always respected these rules, at least as convincingly as the other competing types of political parties in

Europe. Social Democratic parties participate in the contest for
governing power on the basis of their conviction that in so doing
a form of democracy is guaranteed and their own claim to social
change can be redeemed. Social democracy means wanting
governing power within the framework of democracy's groundrules.

It is, therefore, justifiable to measure the success of a
Social Democratic party first of all on whether the party succeeds
in coming to power (in exchanging the role of opposition for
that of government) and in so doing, only then creates the
formal and institutional preconditions for shaping and reforming
society.

Of course, there are governing roles and there are governing roles. Endowed with an immense absolute majority in the
House of Commons, the Labour party government in the United
Kingdom between 1945 and 1950 afforded other, substantially
more favorable conditions for Social Democratic social policy
than, for instance, the Italian Social Democratic party's (PSDI)
participation in numerous coalition governments led by Christian
Democratic premiers in Italy. Thus, the following tabulation
takes into account the various forms and the different strengths
of governing by Social Democrats:

Exclusively Social Democratic governments (4 points for
each year);
Social Democrats in a small coalition (3 points for each year);
Social Democratic participation as an equal partner in a
grand coalition or in a collective government (2 points for each
year);
Social Democratic participation as junior partner in a small
coalition (1 point for each year);
Social Democracy in opposition (0 points per year).

An analysis of the parties' participation in government
shows that the division into government socialism and opposition
socialism is a meaningful one. Between the Social Democracies
of Sweden, Norway, and Denmark, which have been vested with
a virtual maximum of governing power, and the Social Democracies
of France and Italy, which have gone practically without any
governing power, there exist essential, principal role differences.
In the three Scandinavian countries, Social Democracy is a
natural party in power; being estranged from power has been
limited to a few exceptions. In the Mediterranean countries,
on the other hand, Social Democracy has been in power only
by way of exception; in France, never throughout the entire
span of the Fifth Republic, until 1981; in Italy, on occasion

TABLE 31: Measure of Governing Power of Social Democratic
Parties[4]

Socialist or Social Democratic Party	Number of Points Given for Govern- ing Power	Number of Years Under Consideration (until and in- cluding 1979)	Power Quotient (points per year)
Sweden (SAP)	126	35	3.6
Norway (A)	112	35	3.2
Denmark (S)	101	35	2.9
Austria (SPÖ)	82	35	2.3
United Kingdom (Lab)	68	35	1.9
Finland (SDP)	56	35	1.6
Switzerland (SPS)	48[++]	35	1.4
Belgium (BSP/PSB)	45	35	1.3
Netherlands (PvdA)	42	34[+]	1.2
Germany (SPD)	36	31	1.2
France (SFIO, PS)	20	34[+]	0.6
Italy (PSDI)	19	33	0.6
Italy (PSI)	20[+++]	35	0.6

[+]In Netherlands and in France beginning 1946, because
until then, a nonpartisan coalition cabinet was in power.

[++]From 1945 and 1953 one point per year, because there
was only one Social Democratic member of the Bundesrat (cabinet);
from 1959 two points per year, because two Social Democratic
members joined the Bundesrat (out of 7).

[+++]From 1945 until 1947 two points, because the PSI was
in government as a great coalition party; from 1963 only one
point per year, because the PSI was only a minor partner in
the cabinet.

only as the lesser ruling party allied with the larger Christian
Democrats.

The group of Mediterranean Social Democracies with a basic
position of opposition socialism must also include Portugal and
Spain. In these two countries, after decades of fascist one-
party rule, it was not until very recently that a legal, free
Social Democracy was able to develop, in Portugal as of 1974
and Spain from 1976 on. Up to then Social Democracy in these
two states acted as an illegal opposition of principle. Despite a
temporary participation in government in Portugal, the Social
Democratic parties of the Iberian peninsula must be numbered

among the parties with an emphasis on opposition socialism, for
the various characteristics of opposition socialism do apply.
There has been an absence of a long, continuous experience
with governing power; an absence of a close interconnection
with a dominant trade union movement; and an absence of a
monopoly or near monopoly on left votes and left traditions.

Other Social Democratic parties, which have a significantly
more intimate experience with governing power, do not show
these deficiencies. For Swedish and Norwegian, Danish and
Austrian, British and Swiss, Belgian, German, and Dutch Social
Democracy, extensive experience in government, extensive interrelations with trade unions, and an extensive monopoly of the
left go hand in hand. Only Finnish Social Democracy has a
certain in-between position: It is experienced in government
but must, contrary to the other government Socialist parties,
compete with a strong Communist party for trade union influence
and workers' votes.

For the British Labour party, the close interconnections
with the trade union movement certainly constituted one of the
causes leading to the splitting off of a portion of its right wing
and the founding of the Social Democratic party. In the eyes
of the party critics who went over to the Social Democratic
party, the Labour party, which had emerged from the trade
union movement, had become rigid in internal party matters and
irrational in interparty affairs through the dominance of the
trade unions, mediated by collective membership. Instead of
competing with the Conservatives and aiming to win the political
middle, the Labour party moved to the left after its electoral
defeat of 1979 and left a vacuum in the center, into which the
Social Democratic party (not belonging to the Socialist International) moved in alliance with the Liberals.

Governing Power and Party Structure

There are structural differences between government
Socialist and opposition Socialist parties. The government
socialist character of a Social Democratic party increases when
the proportion of workers among the voters is maximal, when
this blue-collar base is substantially supplemented by a white-
collar superstructure, and when the denominational barrier is
minimal. [5]

The inclination to government socialism is advanced by a
dialectical "both-and" situation—by the coexistence of a worker's
party and a people's party. Social Democracy would be too weak

to be a natural ruling party were it to be based exclusively on the blue-collar workers. But it would likewise be too weak if it were to try to penetrate the floating voter realm of white-collar workers without the logical base of a large majority within the working class. The Social Democratic parties with the most accentuated government socialist character—the Swedish, Norwegian, Danish, Austrian, and British parties—are first and foremost worker's parties. They represent the overwhelming majority of workers in their countries, and they are not hindered by any serious competition from a Communist party or a Christian labor movement. The challenge from a large Communist party (Finland) or from well-organized Christian trade unions tied to Christian Democratic parties (Belgium and the Netherlands) diminishes the government socialist character.

Social Democratic parties are large people's parties that successfully reach all major social groups, if they do not cease to be worker's parties. The peculiar feature of opposition socialism is precisely that the Social Democracy either is not the country's primary worker's party (Italy and France) or is seriously challenged in this role (Spain and Portugal).

This connection between government success and party structure cannot, however, be assessed one-sidedly. Whether the Mediterranean Social Democracies are opposition socialist because they lack an adequate command of the dialectical "both-and" feat, or whether they are neither worker's parties nor people's parties because they possess too little governing power lends itself to no simple answer. One must proceed from a reciprocal relationship of conditions, not from a one-sided conditionality.

The assumption of a reciprocal conditionality is supported by the development of a membership structure. There are sufficient empirical indications that a Social Democratic party's degree of organization is not directly dependent upon its governing power. The relatively high degree of organization of the two Italian parties and, in comparison, the not nearly so highly developed degree of organization of, for instance, the Danish or the Norwegian Social Democracy contradict the assumption that government socialism absolutely must have a favorable impact upon the number of members.

The assumption of a simple relationship is also refuted by the development of membership figures for the government Socialist parties; these figures increase or even decrease without any recognizable connection with the party's government role or opposition role. The example of the development of membership in the West German Social Democratic party (SPD)

TABLE 32: Development of Membership of the SPD and the
Labour Party[6]

Number of Members				
			Labour	
			All	Individual
	SPD		Members	Members
1946	711,000	1945	3,038,697	487,047
1954	585,000	1954	6,498,027	933,657
1960	649,000	1960	6,328,330	790,192
1969	778,000	1969	6,163,882	680,656
1972	954,000	1972	6,168,772	703,030
1974	957,000	1974	6,518,457	691,889
1977	1,021,000	1975	6,468,874	674,905

seems to speak for a causal parallelism between government
power and organizational strength; the membership of the German
Social Democrats actually increased significantly when (after
nearly two decades in opposition) the SPD gained power, first
in the context of a grand coalition (1966-69) and finally as the
dominant party in a small coalition (from 1969 on). The membership development in the British Labour party, on the other
hand, took the opposite course. When the party again came to
power after a long period of opposition, the number of individual
members suddenly declined. Social Democratic ruling power can
also turn away members.

A causal relation between the electorate structure and
governing power of Social Democracy is just as ambiguous.
Social Democracy in power can perhaps both produce a fellow-
traveler effect and, by disappointing expectations, turn away
supporters. A Social Democracy in opposition can, by its theoretical consistency, unencumbered by any practice, more firmly
bind sympathizers to the organization; but it can also gradually
lose its supporters by its incapacity for power.

The relation between party structure and governing power
is also complicated by the necessity of explicating the concept
of governing power. Governing power, of course, means first
and foremost the legal exercise of governing authority in the
central government. However, the vertical division of powers
also confers governing power below the national level, even if
it is in opposition in the national parliament, Social Democracy
can hold power at the level of the federal states or municipalities.

Even independently of participation in the federal government, the states, or the local communities, the power question

is still relevant. A Social Democratic party, such as the British Labour party, is still influential because of its close interconnections with the trade unions, even when it is in opposition in the House of Commons and in the most important municipalities. The Labour party and all union-allied Social Democrats have a field of influence here that cannot be comprehended with notions of power defined simply in terms of government.[7]

Austrian Social Democracy, through its ties with the mostly Social Democratic-oriented unions and the binding social partnership of the Austrian Trade Union Federation, takes part indirectly in the exercise of central power even in periods of opposition. In the four years in which the Austrian Socialist party (SPÖ) was in opposition (1966-70), there existed a kind of limited coalition for economic and social policy between the Austrian People's party then in power and the socialist trade unions.[8]

These various possibilities for participating in power do not allow for any unambiguous conclusions on the structure of membership. However, they alter nothing of the fact that the decisive goal of Social Democracy is winning a majority in the central parliament through victory at the polls. Even if the question as to the distribution of political power is no zero-sum game that knows only winners and losers, for Social Democracy a parliamentary majority and thus government is indeed the decisive instrument for establishing a social order in accord with its goals.

This goal also influences the theoretical self-image (that is the ideology and party programs) of Social Democracy. Government experience and ideology have a mutual interdependence. This can be expressed in an exclusion from governing power, prompting a rethinking about party program, which then in turn makes possible electoral success and participation in government. This connection can, however, come about in the opposite way. A Social Democracy in power changes its theory, which is occasioned by its government practice, in order to avoid any all-too gaping inconsistency between the government practice of today and a theory originating in the period of opposition. There are examples of both forms. The SPD model is where government practice follows the theory. After three disappointing elections (1949, 1953, and 1957), the SPD adopted a new program (Godesberg Program) in 1959, anticipating a government pragmatism. The program was a contributing factor in gradually changing the public image of German Social Democracy in such a way that in the coming elections it fared better and thus became capable of governing.[9] The SPÖ model

is where the theory follows government practice. After 1945
Austrian Social Democracy, in the context of the "Grand Coalition," was becoming a party with a government socialist orientation. Yet, there prevailed in the party an opposition socialist
thinking, expressed in the Austro-Marxist Linz Program of
1926; finally, the SPÖ adapted ideology to its practice through
its program of 1958.[10]

Governing Power and Social Structure

   In their development after 1945, the countries with government Socialist parties exhibited a striking democratic continuity
and stability. After the Second World War, none of these
countries experienced a suspension of or even a serious threat
to their constitutional institutions. Politically motivated violence
was limited to isolated phenomena; never was it expressed in
such forms as a civil war or a putsch.
   Such an extensive, continuous peaceful development over
a period of nearly half a century in so many countries is quite
uncommon in Europe's historical experience. The remarkable
aspect of this development becomes clear when one compares
this history with that of the Mediterranean's more strongly
opposition socialist countries; Spain and Portugal were holdovers
from the heyday of European fascism before Western democracy,
before the multiparty system and parliamentarianism, and before
social democracy could develop openly. French democracy was
and is governed by the drastic change of democratic structures
in the course of the transition from the Fourth to the Fifth
Republic in 1958.[11] This change of constitution also meant a
change in the party system; it signified an end to the strongly
government socialist role of the French Socialists and the beginning of their role of permanent opposition. Italy certainly was
not marked by such a decisive break, but the troubles with the
constitutional system of democracy reached such an extent that
after 1945 the stabilized systems of Northern, Central, and
Western Europe have remained unknown.
   Thus, government socialism falls on fertile ground in systems that are stable; in unsettled systems the basic conditions
are rather unfavorable for government socialism. Government
socialism is a consequence and component of democratic stability
and continuity; it is an essential feature of Western democracy.
   Yet, social democracy wanted governing power not for its
own sake; it did not want stable conditions as an end in itself,
but it wanted the restructuring of social relations. For social

democracy it is of no intrinsic value that political peace and democratic order are better developed in countries marked by government socialism than in other countries. Social democracy must ask itself what it has started with these instruments and how it has impressed its stamp upon society.

The declared goal of all Social Democratic parties is to improve the living conditions of the population, especially of the working people. In this, securing jobs is both a self-evident and central concern of Social Democracy, as it also figures among the basic goals of all the established parties. In fact, between the countries of government socialism and the Mediterranean states one can observe no significant difference in the development of unemployment.

Table 33 shows that some countries dominated by government socialism (Denmark) and some countries influenced by government socialism (Belgium and Finland) exhibit a higher rate of unemployment than the two opposition socialist countries (France and Italy). A direct causal relationship between a Social Democratic government and unemployment cannot be substantiated.

Generally, the same must be stated with just as much caution concerning other spheres of the quality of life. In health care services, which is an important indicator of the quality of life not only in a material sense, the connection between government socialism and social policy is equally insignificant. The difference in medical care exists not between the states of government socialism and the Mediterranean states per se but between the economically developed nations (including France and Italy) and the economically backward countries of the Iberian peninsula.

TABLE 33: Rate of Unemployment, 1980 (in percent)[12]

Unemployed Persons of Working Age (average for the year)			
In Countries Influenced by Government Socialism			
Country	Unemployed	Country	Unemployed
Austria	1.9	United Kingdom	7.4
Belgium	11.8	Netherlands	6.0
Denmark	6.3	Norway	1.6
Finland	4.9	Sweden	1.9
Germany	3.8	Switzerland	0.2
Average rate of these countries: 4.6			
In Countries Influenced by Opposition Socialism			
France	6.2	Italy	7.6
Average rate of these countries: 6.9			

TABLE 34: Health Care[13]

Number of Persons Per Physician (P) and Per Hospital Bed (H)

In Countries Influenced by Government Socialism					
	P	H		P	H
Austria (1976)	444	88	United Kingdom (1974)	761	117
Belgium (1976)	493	111	Netherlands (1976)	601	99
Denmark (1976)	512	103	Norway (1976)	567	68
Finland (1976)	703	65	Sweden (1975)	580	66
Germany (1976)	503	84	Switzerland (1976)	524	87
Average rate of these countries: 568.8 (P), 88.8 (H)					
In Countries Influenced by Opposition Socialism					
	P	H		P	H
France (1976)	678	97	Portugal (1976)	817	187
Italy (1974)	502	94	Spain (1976)	545	190
Average rate of these countries: 635.5 (P), 142.0 (H)					

Medical services in France and Italy are basically at the level of
those in the countries of Northern, Central, and Western Europe.

Social democratic social policy can more readily be discerned
in the area of social policy defined in material terms. In the
distribution of incomes, the countries of government socialism
(most of all Sweden) have secured an above average share for
the wage sector and, thus, for the income of workers dependent
on wages. The long-term increase in the wage share means a
relative material betterment for blue-collar and white-collar
workers; it signifies a gradual change of society in the direction
of the employee, which also provides more material privileges
for the general class of employees.

That this material betterment of working people is no acci-
dent but rather the product of a consciously directed social
policy is demonstrated by a comparative examination of the
politically directed application of the national product. In those
countries in which governing Social Democratic parties have
substantially forced up the wage share in cooperation with the
trade unions and favored by other factors, a higher portion
of the national product tends to be redistributed by the state
and, thus, to be withdrawn from direct private consumption.
Sweden is again the country showing the highest percentages
here.

This social impact of a Social Democratic government cannot
be attributed to economic development, as for instance with
health care policy. Economically far more developed states (such
as Switzerland), which are definitely of a weaker government

TABLE 35: Development of Wage Share[14]

Distribution of National Income (nominally)

(percent for wages)		Power Quotient*
Countries Influenced by Government Socialism		
Austria (1979)	73.5	2.3
Belgium (1978)	71.8	1.3
Denmark (1976)	73.3	2.9
Finland (1978)	75.7	1.6
Germany (1978)	70.8	1.2
Netherlands (1978)	72.7	1.2
Norway (1978)	83.0	3.2
Sweden (1978)	89.8	3.6
Switzerland (1977)	67.5	1.4
United Kingdom (1978)	78.5	1.9
Average rate of these countries:	75.7	
Countries Influenced by Opposition Socialism		
France (1978)	70.2	0.6
Italy (1978)	68.3	0.6
Portugal (1976)	68.8	0.0
Spain (1978)	63.6	0.0
Average rate of these countries:	67.7	

*See Table 31.

socialist cast than say Sweden or Denmark or even the United Kingdom, have a significantly lower wage share and an equally clearly lower government share. The clear difference between government socialist and opposition socialist countries also pertains to the economically developed, opposition socialist nations (such as France and Italy). It is not economic development per se that is behind the differences between government socialism and opposition socialism but rather government guided by social policy.

That social democratic economic policy is not simply a consequence of an uncontrolled growth without direct political influence is demonstrated by the inflation rates of the European national economies. In the 1970s the inflation rate of the French economy was above the European average, while the inflation rate of the Italian economy was roughly at the European average. Government and opposition socialism show no connection with the general growth data of the economy.[16]

In some sectors European Social Democracy has been able to fully exercise power in ways that help change and shape

society. In particular, it has progressively raised the material
living conditions of the socially weak, whose interests it took
up at a historical juncture. Of course, this is not a simple
black and white scheme of things. The material conditions of
wage workers are not critically or drastically worse in the economically developed France of the Fifth Republic, which is not
government socialist, than in the likewise developed Sweden,
which is shaped by a governing Social Democracy. There are
recognizable, significant differences, but they do not apply to
a world of those liberated by social democracy and a world of
those exploited by capitalism. The differences are rather
gradated; they relate to grey areas of a gradual material improve-
ment at different rates of development.

That Social Democracy does direct society, when as the
party in power it can utilize the state apparatus, is shown by
Table 37, depicting differential social access to the universities
in Europe. This same table shows that social democracy cannot
direct to the extent that was originally claimed and originally
expected. Everywhere in Europe there is still inequality of
opportunity in the educational system; everywhere in Europe

TABLE 36: Application of National Product [15]

National Product Consumption by the State (in percent)		Power Quotient*
Countries Influenced by Government Socialism		
Austria (1979)	18.1	2.3
Belgium (1978)	17.9	1.3
Denmark (1978)	24.3	2.9
Finland (1978)	19.0	1.6
Germany (1978)	19.9	1.2
Netherlands (1978)	18.3	1.2
Norway (1978)	18.5	3.2
Sweden (1978)	28.9	3.6
Switzerland (1978)	12.9	1.4
United Kingdom (1978)	20.3	1.9
Average rate of these countries:	19.8	
Countries Influenced by Opposition Socialism		
France (1978)	15.1	0.6
Italy (1978)	16.5	0.6
Portugal (1976)	14.2	0.0
Spain (1978)	10.6	0.0
Average rate of these countries:	14.1	

*See Table 31.

TABLE 37: Social Filters in European Universities[17]

Changes of Social Impediments in Countries Influenced by Government Socialism		
Sweden - Percentage of blue-collar workers' children who are freshmen at universities	1962	1972
Male	17.6	25.2
Female	14.7	21.0
Germany - Percentage of students at universities with lower-class fathers	1967	1973
	7.8	13.0
Netherlands - Percentage of students at universities with lower-class origin	1961	1970
	11.0	14.0
Austria - Percentage of blue-collar workers' children who are freshmen at universities	1967	1977
Male	14.8	12.5
Female	9.1	10.4
Changes of Social Impediments in a Country Influenced by Opposition Socialism		
France - Percentage of students at universities with manual worker fathers	1967	1971
	11.1	12.6

it is particularly the wage workers, the core strata of the labor movement and of social democracy, who are disadvantaged in their chances for social advancement. But social democracy has been able to ameliorate this disadvantage and break down injustice.

The sociopolitical truth of European Social Democracy rests in the middle. It has not eliminated class society in such a way that materially and immaterially measurable discrimination has ceased to exist and that a classless, just, and egalitarian society has emerged. But social democracy has shaped politics and society in terms of the progressive reformism of the pragmatic archheretic Eduard Bernstein.

If one simply imagines that there are no Social Democratic parties in today's Europe, then the product of this fiction is not simply mass misery and mass oppression. Even without social democracy there is democracy; even without social democracy there is social balance, social security, and social welfare. Social democracy is not a political force that can or wants to act

fundamentally differently from the other important forces of
Europe; it is a force that makes policy somewhat differently and
that changes society a little.[18]

DOMESTIC POLITICAL ALLIANCES

The way in which powers are connected within a parliamentary system makes any form of governing dependent on the
creation of a parliamentary majority. Only in exceptional cases
are Social Democratic parties in a position to establish this
majority on their own and then to govern on their own. In
these cases questions of alliance policy are superfluous. In all
other cases the search for an ally in parliament and government
and the planning and realization of coalitions is part and parcel
of Social Democratic politics.

Social Democratic one-party governments, which render
parliamentary alliances and government coalitions superfluous,
come about under the following conditions:

A Social Democratic parliamentary majority, based on an
electoral system that fosters majorities

A Social Democratic parliamentary majority, in spite of a
proportional electoral system that does not favor majorities

Social Democratic minority governments, based on the
tolerance of parties to the right or left of the Social Democrats

The first is the British case. Indeed the British Labour
party has been able many times to gain an absolute majority in
the House of Commons (1945, 1950, 1964, 1966, and 1970); however, it has always managed to do so with only a plurality of
the vote. The reinforcing effect of the plurality election turned
the relative voter majority into an absolute parliamentary majority
and secured the basis for a Social Democratic government.

The second is the Scandinavian-Austrian case. Despite
proportional voting, the Social Democrats gained absolute parliamentary majorities in Norway (1945, 1949, 1953, and 1957),
Sweden (1968), and Austria (1971, 1975, and 1979). The Social
Democrats won an absolute majority of the vote only in Sweden
and Austria. In Norway they achieved an absolute parliamentary
majority with a plurality of the votes.[19]

The third case of a solely Social Democratic government
is also a Scandinavian-Austrian phenomenon. The Finnish
Social Democrats (1948 and 1972), the Norwegian Social Democrats (1961, 1963, 1971, 1973, and 1977), the Austrian Social

Democrats (1970), the Swedish Social Democrats (1945, 1946, 1957, and 1970) and the Danish Social Democrats (1947, 1950, 1953, 1955, 1962, 1964, 1967, 1971, 1975, and 1977) formed one-party governments without parliamentary majorities. This pattern of government, which is almost the rule in Denmark, Norway, and Sweden, was complemented by the minority government of the Socialist party of Portugal (1976-78).[20]

However, Social Democratic minority governments emanate from an indirect, implicit alliance politics. Without a stable majority, Social Democratic parties do not launch into the adventure of forming a government without agreements or without the plausible expectation of support from one other party. Thus, in their numerous minority governments, the Danish Social Democrats often relied on the Liberals and the Swedish Social Democrats on the Communists. The SPÖ governed between 1970 and 1971 on the basis of a parliamentary agreement with the Freedom party of Austria.

Thus, minority governments are part and parcel of Social Democratic alliance strategies. Just like the nature and extent of open coalition governments, they can provide information about the possibilities and limits of social democracy.

Directions of Alliance Policy

In the European multiparty system, Social Democracy vies with different party groupings. However, one can distinguish two fundamental directions to this interparty rivalry: competition on the right and competition on the left.

For Social Democracy the competition on the right consists in the struggle with Conservative, Christian Democratic, Liberal, and other bourgeois parties. The opposition to these right-wing parties has a socioeconomic and sociopsychological foundation— the bourgeois parties have a different social structure, which is often complemented by a different denominational structure.

For Social Democracy the competition on the left consists chiefly in the struggle with Communist parties in addition to left Socialist parties. These parties are distinguished from the Social Democrats partly by a different understanding of democracy (Communists without the turn to Eurocommunism) and partly by an emphatically socialist consistency (Eurocommunism and left socialism).

The alliance policy of Social Democracy vis-à-vis these rival parties is in no way uniform. In many states the Social Democrats seek alliances exclusively with parties on the right

(Belgium, the Netherlands, the Federal Republic of Germany, Switzerland, and Austria). In many states Social Democrats orient alliance policy both to the left and to the right (Finland and Denmark, but also in Italy, Spain, and Portugal). An unequivocal preference for a left-oriented alliance policy can be detected only in France.

Since 1945 the Belgian Socialist party (BSP-PSB), with quite remote prospects for governing on its own, has formed a variety of governing alliances, mainly with the Christian Democratic Christelijke Volkspartij/Parti Social Chrétien (CVP-PSC), but also with the Liberal Partides Reformes et de la Liberté de Wallonie (PRLW) and with the two regional parties, the Flemish People's Union and the Rassemblement Wallon.

The German Social Democrats have had alliance experience both with the Christlich-Demokratische Union/Christlich-Soziale Union (CDU-CSU) and with the Liberal Freie Demokratische Partei (FDP). After the long period of opposition, however, the government alliance with the Christian Democrats marked only a transition to the long-term government alliance with the Liberals.

After 1945 the Danish Social Democrats have had an open government alliance on the right (with the left-liberal Radical Venstre and with the right-liberal Venstre) and a tacit alliance on the left (minority government supported in parliament by the Left Socialists-Socialist People's party).

This Scandinavian model of a two-sided alliance policy also characterizes the weakest Social Democracy of Scandinavia, the Social Democratic party of Finland. Unlike the Danish Social Democrats, the Finns form coalitions with the right (chiefly the Center) and the left (Communists) at the same time, and thus they often become the focal point of a broad, comprehensive coalition, which practically assumes the character of a collective government.

In the Fifth Republic, the Socialist party of France brought about an alliance of the entire left opposition as an alternative coalition. In view of the difference in size between the Communists and the small left-liberal Radical Socialists, this alliance is an alliance on the left, in the tradition of the French Popular Front government (1936-38).

Following the coalition government necessitated by the war, the British Labour party entered into neither a government nor an opposition alliance. The British two-party system is basically set up in such a way that alliances are not meaningful and are also not common. However, one parliamentary alliance in support of the Labour government was the agreement with the Liberal

TABLE 38: Orientation of Social Democratic Alliances After 1945[1]

	Cooperation of Social Democratic Parties on Different Levels		
	Cabinet (coalitions)	Parliament (minority cabinets)	Outside Parliament (electoral alliances)
Austria (SPÖ)	right (CD)	right (RL)	—
Belgium (BSP/PSB)	right (especially CD)	—	—
Denmark (S)	right (especially LL)	left (especially LS)	—
Finland (SDP)	right and left (especially C and Comm.)	right and left	—
France (PS)	right and left (LL and Comm.)	—	right and left (LL and Comm.)
Germany (SPD)	right (especially L)	—	—
Italy (PSI)	right (especially CD)	right and left (especially CD and Comm.)	left (especially Comm.)
Italy (PSDI)	right (especially CD)	right and left (especially CD and Comm.)	—
Netherlands (PvdA)	right (especially CD)	—	—
Norway (A)	left (LS)	left (especially LS)	—
Portugal (PS)	right (CD)	right and left (Comm., L, CD)	right (especially Con.)
Spain (PSOE)	—	—	—
Sweden (SAP)	right (especially C, L)	left (especially Comm.)	right and left (especially C and Comm.)
Switzerland (SPS)	right (CD, L, Con.)	—	—
United Kingdom (Lab)	—	right (especially L)	—

Note: CD = Christian Democrats; Comm. = Communists; Con. = Conservatives; C = Center party; L = Liberals; LL = Left Liberals; RL = Right Liberals; LS = Left Socialists.

party between 1976 and 1978, which guaranteed the Callaghan government the majority that the Labour party, following several defeats in byelections, was no longer able to secure by itself.

For Italian Social Democracy, the alliance question became a question of survival. The split between the Italian Socialist party (PSI) and the PSDI, effected in 1947 and again, after a brief period of reunification, in 1969, was inflamed, chiefly by this question. The PSI had, at least in 1947, a clear preference for a left alliance; the PSDI clearly leaned toward a right alliance. For the 1948 elections the PSI formed an opposition alliance with the Communists with the explicit intention of governing jointly with them following an electoral victory. Of course, after this strategy misfired, the Socialist partiality toward such an alliance cooled, but the PSI was unable to decide on any inclination toward the right, at least nothing unequivocal. Today the alliance and coalition issue remains a significant difference between the two Socialist or Social Democratic parties of Italy. The PSDI is anti-Communist and is clearly oriented toward agreements with the Christian Democrats and with the other small parties of the center; the PSI demonstrates an openness toward both the Christian Democrats and the Communists.[22]

The Dutch Labor party (PvdA) has known only alliances on the right since 1945. Governing agreements with the denominational parties, particularly with the Catholic People's party as well as with smaller parties of the center, have made possible various coalition governments, which have been shared by the Social Democrats. However, the alliance on the left has been more important for Social Democracy in Norway. Between 1963 and 1965 the Labor party governed jointly with the Socialist People's party (left Socialists); later on Social Democratic minority governments were supported in parliament by the left Socialists. The Social Democrats' willingness to enter into alliances on the right has been expressed only in extraparliamentary fashion, when the Conservative party was the only grouping to support the Social Democrats' policy in favor of admission to the European Economic Community and when it organized a substantial portion of the pro-Europe votes in the defeated referendum of 1972.

The Austrian SPÖ has known only alliances on the right. The "Grand Coalition" between 1945 and 1966 was a governing alliance; the parliamentary arrangement with the right-liberal/ German-national Freiheitliche Partei Österreichs (FPÖ) in support of the Socialist minority government of 1970-71 was a parliamentary alliance. These have been the concrete forms of the SPÖ's basic strategic orientations.

Since the reestablishment of democracy and the multiparty system in 1974, the Socialist party of Portugal has been open to political alliances on the left and the right. Between 1976 and 1978 the Socialist minority government relied partly upon ad hoc arrangements with the parties of the right and partly on agreement with the Communists. In 1978 the Socialist party entered into a brief governing coalition with the center Democrats.

The Swedish Social Democratic party has been characterized in part by attempts to keep alive Social Democratic minority governments by means of parliamentary alliances (primarily with the Communists) and in part by government alliances toward the right (chiefly with the center and the Liberals). Thus, the Scandinavian pattern of being open to both sides applies here again in the case of Sweden.

Social Democrats in Switzerland have known only alliances on the right. Since 1959 the confederative model of a collective government has regularly included Social Democracy; all other parties in power are parties of the right competition.

In the brief span of its legal activity since 1976, the Socialist Workers' party of Spain (PSOE) has entered into neither a government alliance with the ruling Democratic Center nor an opposition alliance with the Communists, say on the French model. The PSOE placed an accent on alliance politics through its accession to the Moncloa Pact, with which the government and the large opposition parties attempted in October 1977 to close ranks in a social partnership. Thus, Spanish Social Democracy shows a cautious alliance orientation, open at both sides.

The alliance policies of the various Social Democratic parties reveal very few principles. A consistent anti-Communism in the form of a rejection of any tactical or strategic arrangement with Communists is evident in only a few cases (Austria and the Federal Republic of Germany). A consistent rejection of alliances on the right is nowhere in evidence; the only manifest rejection on principle is the exclusion of the Italian neofascists Movimento Sociale Italiano-Destra Nazionale (MSI-DN) from all parliamentary agreements, an exclusion that is only natural for the two Italian Social Democratic parties. Alliance policy in the government, in the parliament, and outside the parliament is ultimately not a question of principle at all but rather a question of possibility and utility.

Determinants of Alliance Policy

Whether a Social Democratic party enters into a government alliance with a Liberal or Conservative party; whether a Social

TABLE 39: Determinants of Social Democratic Alliances[23]

Average Electoral Strength (percent of votes in general elections) from 1945 until the Middle of the 1970s

	Competition on the Right			Social Democracy		Left Competition	
	1	2	3	1	2	1	2
Austria	52.3	7	no	44.9	2	3.0	9
Belgium	53.7	5	no	31.6	7	4.8	7
Denmark	45.7	11	yes	37.1	5	10.8	4
Finland	42.7	12	yes	24.8	10	22.4	3
France (since 1958)	60.5	2	no	15.2	12	24.3	2
Germany	53.7	5	no	31.6	6	2.7	11
Italy (PSI and PSDI)	55.3	4	no	19.7	11	27.1	1
Netherlands	55.3	3	no	28.3	8	4.8	7
Norway	47.7	10	yes	44.2	4	8.5	5
Sweden	49.0	9	yes	46.4	1	5.7	6
Switzerland	66.7	1	yes	25.4	9	2.8	10
United Kingdom	52.0	8	no	44.4	3	0.2	12

Note: 1 = Average percent of votes in general elections—only stabilized parties considered, not splinter parties or parties with a short-term existence; 2 = Position compared with percent in other countries; 3 = Fragmentation of right competition; fragmented (yes) means that there is no dominant party on the right.

Democratic minority government relies on the votes of the left Socialists or the Communists in parliament; whether a Social Democratic party enters into an opposition alliance with the Communists—all are related to several factors: the magnitude of the Social Democracy, the magnitude of the right opposition, the magnitude of the left opposition, or the homogeneity of the right opposition.

The greater the weight of the Social Democratic party itself, the less willing it is to enter into the most intensive form of alliance (the governing alliance) and the more willing it is to form a Social Democratic-dominated government alliance with smaller parties of the right opposition. It is more willing as well to accept the support of the left opposition in parliament for a minority government.

The stronger the competition from the right, the lower the probability of an alliance of Social Democracy with right-wing parties and the higher the probability of an alternative opposition alliance on the left.

The weightier the left-wing parties, the greater the willingness of Social Democracy to seek government alliances, parliamentary arrangements, or extraparliamentary ties with Communists or left Socialists and the less the possibility for Social Democracy to accord a clear priority to alliances on the right.

The more pronounced the fragmentation of the parties to the right of Social Democracy and the better the Social Democratic party's basis for alliance policy, the more likely the willingness to form small coalitions with a part of the right and the greater the willingness also to form minority governments, secured by a part of the right opposition or the left opposition.

Despite these varying influences, the alliance policy of Social Democracy can be reduced to four basic models of action. The British model of Social Democratic alliance policy basically excludes alliances altogether, accepting them only as emergency solutions in times of war or in transitional phases, when the situation as to parliamentary majority is not clear.

The Scandinavian model of Social Democratic alliance policy implies an equivalence of alliances left and right and frequently leads to Social Democratic minority governments, based on parliamentary support from the left or right.

The Central European model of Social Democratic alliance policy (the Netherlands, Belgium, Germany, Switzerland, and Austria) is oriented exclusively to alliances on the right and largely excludes the Communists from all alliance considerations on principle.

The Southern European model of Social Democratic alliance policy means openness to both sides, whereby this openness is less government oriented (as in Scandinavia) and more opposition oriented, geared to confrontations with right-wing governments.

The alliance policy of Social Democracy is determined by practice and not by theory. Social Democracy needs agreements; it needs partners in order to be able to realize its claims. In this striving to be able to make policy, and that means primarily to be able to govern, the Social Democratic parties of the present are to a great extent inclined toward pragmatism and flexibility.

The alliance policy of the individual parties differs a great deal. Common to them all is the fact that they regard alliances purposively; that the pull toward governing and government power is often stronger than all principles; and that the desire, therefore, to be able to govern becomes the most important principle of Social Democratic alliance policy.

INTERRELATIONS WITH ASSOCIATIONS

The history of the Social Democratic worker's movement is also the history of Social Democratic trade unions. Social Democratic parties, as the democratically legitimated, parliament-oriented arm of the worker's movement, were always complemented by Social Democratic unions, which influenced the political decision-making process in the preparliamentary arena. The party was to carry on politics in the state, while the union conducted politics in the society—harmonized and complementary.

This matter-of-course relationship, which Victor Adler described as that of Siamese twins[24] was self-evident only in the integral Marxist stage of social democracy. In many countries the unions have pulled out of the embrace of the Social Democratic parties. The marriage between Social Democratic parties and Social Democratic-dominated trade unions has been jeopardized above all by two developments. The split in the Social Democratic worker's movement into a communist and a Social Democratic direction also split the trade union movement. Everywhere there emerged a rivalry between Social Democratic and Communist trade union politics, a rivalry that in some cases also destroyed the unions.[25] Christian trade unions, especially Catholic unions, likewise developed into rivals of Social Democratic unions. In every country in which political Catholicism was able to exert a substantial influence on the party landscape, Catholic unions played an important role as rivals of the Social Democrats (chiefly in the Benelux countries but also in France and Italy).[26]

Even in the last quarter of the twentieth century, a great deal of importance is ascribed to the relations of the parties of the Socialist International with trade unions. The unions can be the essential factor of support for Social Democracy, but they can also be a hindrance as a negative structural condition for Social Democracy. The scope of institutional and personal interrelations between unions and Social Democratic parties; the fundamental orientation of trade union strategy, which is the strength of its readiness to engage in conflict; the degree of trade union organization; and the institutional as well as ideological homogeneity of the unions are important defining quantities of social democratic policy.[27]

Compared to the significance of the relationship between Social Democratic parties and trade unions, the relationship between Social Democracy and other associations is of only secondary importance. Of course, it is not unimportant for a Social Democratic party to maintain contact with, say, employer's

associations or farmer's associations; surely, these and other
associations can influence the conditions for Social Democratic
success. But trade union politics are addressed first and foremost to the Social Democratic parties, and the trade unions are
the most important potential allies of Social Democratic parties.

Relations between Social Democracy
and Trade Unions

Between a trade union movement and a political party there
are three possible kinds of relations.[28] A unitary trade union
concentrates its contacts with one party (the British model);
a unitary trade union entertains relations with several parties,
with priority given to contacts with one party (the German and
Austrian models); or several trade unions (alignment unions)
maintain relations with several parties (the Italian, French,
Belgian, and Dutch models).
The structuring of relations between trade unions and
Social Democracy in Denmark, Finland, and Sweden can be
considered a Scandinavian mixed model. A unitary trade union,
which especially in Denmark and Sweden is closely interrelated
with Social Democracy, is challenged by a relatively strong
white-collar union, which extricates itself from the unitary claim
of the umbrella organization. Here elements of the British model
(Denmark and Sweden) and the German and Austrian models
(Finland) are mixed with the structures of alignment unions,
whereby the criterion of the alignment unions is not that of a
world view or a class struggle but that of social status (white-
collar or blue-collar).
However, in these cases of a coexistence of a unitary trade
union and a status-oriented, white-collar union, it is always
Social Democracy that has the best ties with the unions and
often has a close personal and institutional synchronization with
the unions. With important qualifications, the trade union situation in the Federal Republic of Germany can also be included
under this Scandinavian mode. The Deutsche Angestelltenge-
werkschaft (DAG), outside the German Trade Union Federation
(DGB), is admittedly weaker than the analogous white-collar
unions in the Scandinavian countries. But like these it is not
a political or ideological alignment union; it is—like the DGB
and the white-collar unions of Scandinavia—partially linked to
Social Democracy through personal ties.[29]
The position of Social Democracy in relation to the unions
is at its weakest where there is a system of alignment unions

based on denomination or party ties, that is in Belgium, France, Italy, and—with some qualifications—in the Netherlands and Spain. In the Netherlands the Social Democratic-dominated alignment union Nederlands Verbond van Vakverenigingen (NVV) and in Spain the Socialist-dominated alignment union Union General de Trabajo (UGT) represent the strongest of the trade union associations. Moreover, in the Netherlands since 1975, there has been an umbrella organization that links the Catholic alignment unions with the NVV. In Belgium the Christian Democratic trade union federation Confédération des Syndicats Chrétien (CSC) is stronger than the Social Democratic alignment union Fédération Générale du Travail de Belgique (FGTB).[30]

The weakest position vis-à-vis the trade unions in general is that of Social Democracy in France and Italy.[31] In France the Socialist party (PS) does have traditionally close contacts with the trade union association Force Ouvriére (FO), whose base is chiefly civil servants and white-collar workers. Moreover, for some years the PS has had good connections with the previously Christian Democratic, now more left-socialist trade union association Confédération Francaise Démocratique du Travail (CFDT), which however demonstrates its independence from political parties by prohibiting its officials from holding any party office. Far and away the strongest alignment union of France Confédération Générale du Travail (CGT) is de facto a Communist trade union movement.

In Italy trade union activists of the PSI represent both a minority in the Communist-directed alignment union Confederazione Generale Italiana del Lavoro (CGIL) and a group within the third-strongest union association Unione Italiana del Lavoro (UIL), which is traditionally Socialist-Social Democratic-Republican. Social Democrats of the PSDI are also in the UIL association. The strongest forces determining trade union politics are thus not in any way bound to Social Democracy in Italy or in France.

The politics of trade unions can be analyzed through systematic observation of their conflict behavior. Unions can be divided into conflict types and cooperation types, with the frequency of labor conflicts as the gauge. Conflict-type unions attempt to realize their demands through open conflicts. Their willingness to engage in conflict reflects a fundamental distance from the existing political and social order. An indicator of conflict-type behavior is a remarkable frequency of strikes. Cooperation-type unions attempt to realize their demands by way of negotiating and convincing. In general they are largely bound to the existing order; an indicator of their behavior is a low frequency of strikes.

TABLE 40: Conflict Behavior of Unions and Relations Between Unions and Social Democracy[32]

	Strike Minutes Per Employee				Organizational Degree+ (in percent)	Degree of Linkage	Power Quotient++
	1976	1977	1978	1979			
Austria	0.0	0.0	2.0	0.0	58-60	3	2.3
Belgium	139.0	103.0	156.0	96.0	65-70	1	1.3
Denmark	51.5	55.5	30.0	40.5	60-70	3	2.9
Finland	325.0	630.0	35.5	65.5	65-80	2	1.6
France	141.0	102.0	61.0	+++	23-25	1	0.6
Germany	12.5	0.5	97.5	11.0	35-40	3	1.2
Italy	876.5	562.0	345.5	935.0	33-40	1	0.6
Netherlands	1.5	29.0	0.5	37.5	35	3	1.2
Norway	43.5	7.5	19.0	2.0	55	3	3.2
Spain	690.0	915.0	653.0	1069.5	+++	2	0.0
Sweden	3.0	11.0	4.5	3.5	85	3	3.6
Switzerland	4.0	1.0	1.0	0.5	25-30	2	1.4
United Kingdom	70.0	215.0	199.0	624.0	45-50	3	1.9

+Organizational degree refers to the number of unionized workers' as a percent of all employees.

++See Table 31.

+++Data not yet available. Also no data published for strike frequency in Portugal.

Note: Degree of linkage refers to the intensity of relations between unions and Social Democracy.
3: Unitary trade union dominated by a Social Democratic party; 2: Leading alignment union dominated by Social Democrats or important but not dominating role of Social Democrats inside unitary trade union. 1: Dominating role of Social Democrats in smaller alignment unions only or no leading influence of Social Democrats on unions at all.

Strike frequency, of course, cannot be attributed one-sidedly to trade union conduct. Behind every strike statistic there is also the conduct of the other side—the employers and their associations. Frequent strikes speak not only of conflict-oriented behavior on the part of the unions but just as much of conflict-oriented behavior by the employers. Strike statistics are indicators of the intensity of conflict between capital and labor and of the extent of satisfaction with the existing social order in general.

There does exist a clear relationship between the trade unions' doubly explicable willingness to engage in conflict, on the one hand, and the texture of trade union organization, the interrelations between unions and Social Democracy, and the governing power of Social Democratic parties, on the other. The greater the proportion of union-organized workers in the aggregate of wage workers in a country, the stronger the link between unions and Social Democracy, and the more powerful Social Democracy is in terms of participation in government, the greater the probability of a cooperative stance on the part of the unions.

The influence of Social Democratic parties on the state (defined as influence on the government) and on society (defined as influence on the unions) attenuates social conflicts, mitigating the contradiction between labor and capital. The fundamental conflict typical of the capitalist social order, expressed in the confrontation of trade unions and employer associations, is in no way eliminated by European Social Democracy, but it is mitigated.

This clear picture is clouded by only one exception, though a very important one: the United Kingdom and the conflict behavior of the British trade union association Trade Union Congress (TUC). The British trade unions are recognized as being among the most conflict-oriented, although they are closely interconnected with the Labour party, and the latter is a government socialist-type party with a high power quotient. There are ample explanations for the causes behind this aberration; in particular, reference must be made to the extremely decentralized structure of the British union system and to the domination of the party structure by the unions. [33]

But beyond the exceptional British case, the fact remains that Social Democracy promotes social peace. The party, which in most European countries has won over a large majority of the workers, exerts a significant dampening effect on the movement's classic means of struggle, the strike. This connection is again, of course, an ambivalent one; it has to be seen dialectically.

The positive connection between social peace and Social Democracy's power in government and in the trade unions can be interpreted as an insidious betrayal by the Social Democrats of the goals of the worker's movement. Accordingly, Social Democracy is a sedative that makes an oppressive social order seemingly tolerable to those it oppresses. Social Democracy's influence in promoting social peace can, however, be interpreted in precisely the opposite way, as the result, in part, of an already completed, fundamental change in social relations. Accordingly, the government and trade union power of Social Democracy has already achieved substantial portions of the goals of the worker's movement; the social peace it promotes is the expression of a justified satisfaction of the working class, which is now no longer exploited or at least no longer exploited in the old way.

The assessment of this influence of Social Democratic power on the politics of the trade unions depends upon the assessment of the social order. Whoever basically accepts the social welfare state of the late twentieth century will also concede the stabilizing influence of the Social Democratic-directed trade unions. Whoever criticizes this social welfare state on principle must also take a negative view of the support for this social order by a powerful but reformist and cooperative union movement.

This negative assessment of the strong yet reformist role of cooperative trade unions under Social Democratic dominance can be a critique from the left or a critique from the right. The reproach to Social Democracy and trade unions—that they place the tactic of negotiating short-term benefits ahead of the strategy of overcoming capitalism—is a criticism from the left. The complaint that the trade unions, supported by Social Democracy, have established the "union state," in which power no longer emanates from the parliament and the other constitutional organs but from the unions and that they have even destroyed the laws of the free market economy is a criticism from the right.

The synchronization between unions and Social Democracy can occur in a twofold way.[34] In the institutional interrelations model, unions as organization are directly and formally linked with Social Democracy as a party. Institutional interrelation is highly developed primarily in Denmark, the United Kingdom, Norway, and Sweden and is also present in Spain. In the personal interrelations model, unions and Social Democracy are as organizations completely independent of one another; however, a synchronization is established through numerous personal cross-connections and through dual functions in the union and in the party. This form of interrelation is highly developed chiefly in Belgium, the Netherlands, the Federal Republic of Germany, Austria, and Switzerland; is weaker in Finland; and is weakest in Italy, France, and Portugal.

A special form of interrelation has developed in the Austrian Trade Union Federation (ÖGB). The ÖGB does, of course, maintain its function as supraparty trade union movement, but it has institutionalized the influence of the party on the union movement in the form of caucuses. By far the strongest caucus is the Socialist caucus, which thus guarantees the influence of the SPÖ on the ÖGB (though, too, the ÖGB's influence on the SPÖ). In this way the personal interrelations are also institutionally secured. As representatives of the Socialist caucus, most of the leading officials of the ÖGB are also Social Democratic party functionaries; a relatively large part of the mandataries placed by the SPÖ in the organs of government comes from the unions. [35]

Fundamental political consonance in maintaining the division of labor between Social Democracy and trade unions is one mark of government socialism. It is primarily in the states characterized by opposition socialism (France, Italy, and Portugal) that the trade union movement is more strongly dominated by the Communists than the Social Democrats. The fundamental harmony between the trade union movement and a large party that is often invested with governing power is largely a feature of the unions in the United States and the Democratic party. The American Federation of Labor-Congress of Industrial Organizations (AFL-CIO) is autonomous; it is not bound to or institutionally interconnected with any party. Nevertheless, the U.S. trade union movement supports the Democratic party in many ways, and the politics of this party is also more amenable to the unions than that of the rival Republican party. If we disregard the labels and the traditions, then the Democratic party of the United States has to be identified as a veiled social democracy of a government socialist orientation precisely because of its close ties with the union movement. [36]

Social Democracy and Grass-roots Organizations

For Social Democracy the unions were and are the most important economic association, the most important organization of any kind with which it shares a relationship of reciprocal sustenance and influence. Beyond that, however, Social Democracy has developed a close mesh of relations with other associations designed to secure the influence of Social Democratic politics in various sectors.

Here the consumer co-operative societies have a special tradition. Co-ops were significant for the development of British, Scandinavian, and Austrian Social Democracy as a socialization factor. This still finds expression today in the collective membership in the Labour party; like membership in the unions, membership in the consumer co-operatives also conveys membership in the Labour party. [37]

The various associations at the grass roots of Social Democracy have unfolded, mainly where the political culture in general as well as the political culture of Social Democracy were marked by segmentation and the camp mentality. The Dutch and the Austrian Social Democrats (in part also the Swiss) formed their own society within a society, their own culture within the culture. This Social Democratic countersystem encompassed numerous cultural and economic organizations offering a corresponding organizational structure for each and every conceivable interest of the Social Democrats, from the athletic club to the educational association, from the student's organization to the pensioner's union. [38]

Austrian Social Democracy, which in the decades of Austro-Marxism (up to 1934) cultivated this Social Democratic counter-culture with particular intensity, today still shows a total of 32 grass-roots organizations as official institutions of the party. This includes the Working Group for Christianity and Socialism as well as the Federation of Working Jews of Austria, the Workers Temperance League of Austria as well as the Austrian Workers Choral Federation, the First Austrian Workers Stamp Collectors Union as well as the Association of Austrian Workers Fishing Clubs, and the League of Socialist Esperantists of Austria. [39]

However, the importance of these grass-roots organizations for party life and the politics of Social Democracy is generally declining. This can be established even where the membership figures for the Social Democratic associations remain high. At the end of the 1970s the membership in Social Democratic consumer cooperatives in Sweden numbered roughly 1.2 million. However, the Social Democratic Workers party has less and less need of this socialization instrument for building consciousness; hence, the political weight of the cooperatives is also declining. [40]

The diminishing role of the Social Democratic club and association life in the individual parties has a similar background as the decline of the Social Democratic press. The highly developed Social Democratic organizations, with a strong existence of their own, were a consequence of the distance and exclusion of the Social Democrats and the working class generally. Precisely through its successes, Social Democracy has led the work-

ing class up to the ruling social order by changing that order.
An autonomous proletarian subculture is thus largely superfluous;
it has been outstripped by history.

On the other hand, structuring relations with the employers'
associations is of increasing importance, again primarily for the
successful, government socialist-oriented parties. Social Democratic parties that are in office or are on the verge of coming to
power must also find a modus vivendi with the industry and
trade associations. However, for this sort of problem there
are no systematic answers in the practice of the individual Social
Democratic parties. The inevitable contacts with these organizations, which are traditionally interconnected with the bourgeois
parties, in general go not via the party but via the government.
In their capacities as heads of government or ministers, Social
Democrats in power attempt to negotiate compromises with the
representatives of the employers' interests. The party as such
is scarcely affected by this directly, though it is indirectly.
Government socialism, then, means to some extent taking into
consideration the interests of the employers and of capital.

A particularly important arena for this form of cautious,
indirect ties to the employers' associations is that of the social
partnership institutions, which the Social Democrats, precisely
in their government function, have had a hand in shaping.
The Concerted Action program in the Federal Republic of Germany
originates with the initiative of Social Democratic Economic
Affairs Minister Karl Schiller; it was designed to bring about
a central agreement on economic policy between government,
unions, and employers. The SPD was involved, not as party
but very much so as government and as dominant group within
the trade unions.[41]

It is the trademark of all successful parties striving for
governing power that they are able to establish a systematic
connection with all possible interest groups. Social Democracy
still confronts this necessity even when it actually exercises
government power. It must also organize contacts with associations whose interests have traditionally been alien to Social
Democracy. The Social Democracy of today is in a transitional
stage: the still primary relations with the trade unions need to
be systematically supplemented by relations with the employer
associations. Against this task, the organizational life in the
area of a Social Democratic subculture recedes into the background. The successful Social Democracy of today needs the
best, most direct possible line to the trade unions. But it has
less and less need for the organizations of its own subculture,
for this subculture is breaking up. It has an increasingly

strong need for communication with the representative interests of capital.

Here, too, the transformation of European Social Democracy is abundantly clear. It has long become an established force; thus, it also ceases to represent an independent politicocultural milieu. It has much more need of contact with all organized forces that could interfere with its rule, even and especially with those forces that traditionally have not been well-disposed toward it.

INTERNATIONAL FEDERATIONS

Internationalism is an essential characteristic of social democracy. The Social Democratic worker's movement from the very start saw itself as the union of the working class above and beyond the borders of nations and states. The history of social democracy is marked by attempts to unite the individual parties worldwide and to harmonize their politics internationally. The history of social democracy is also a history of the Internationals.

The First International was of short duration. It was founded in London in 1864 and dissolved de facto after the Hague Congress in 1872. This International Working Man's Association had to suffer sorely from struggles over direction. Karl Marx took part in formulating its statutes and did compose the inaugural address; but the First International was in no way an instrument in his hands. The conflicts between the individual currents, particularly between Marx and the anarchists, led to a break. The General Council, which removed to New York following the conference in The Hague, now represented little more than a fraction of the organizations originally united; the formal dissolution of the International in Philadelphia in 1876 was scarcely of any importance. [42]

The Second International, founded in 1889, differed substantially from the First International. The various workers movements that were now uniting were in some cases already powerful parties. The Second International was marked not by intellectual professional revolutionaries on the run but by party organizations struggling for power. The largest party at the time the International was founded, the German Social Democracy, captured roughly 20 percent of the vote in the 1890 elections to the German Reichstag; behind it stood more than one million voters. At the time the Second International was founded, the British trade union movement numbered approximately one million workers. [43]

The International now represented real power. The decisive
split in the International emanated, however, precisely from a
party that represented no established power, whose structure
was typical of the situation of the First International. The
Social Democratic party of Russia was a party in exile; of necessity it assessed questions of organization and strategy differently
than the large legal parties of Germany, the United Kingdom,
France, Austria-Hungary, and Italy. The expectation of carrying out a revolution in small steps, by democratizing parliament
and parliamentarizing the state, and the temptation of theoretical
and even more so of practical revisionism had to remain alien to
an outlawed Social Democracy in exile, just as much as this
temptation would have to be obvious to a Social Democracy already
dominating parliaments.

The Second International collapsed under the chauvinism
of the First World War and under the Russian October Revolution.
In 1919, the Communist International was called into being in
Moscow. Behind it stood portions of the old parties of the Second
International. An attempt, by means of a conference in Vienna
in 1921, to create the "Two-and-a-half International" and in
this way mediate between social democracy and communism and
thus save the International was a failure. In 1923 the Second
International was revived under the name of the Labor and
Socialist International; it united all the currents of social democ-
racy not affiliated with the Communist International.[44]

The Labor and Socialist International was the tribune of
social democracy during the interwar period. In 1931 it represented altogether more than 6 million members and more than
26 million voters, nearly all connected with European parties.
By far the strongest were the British Labour party and the
SPD.[45]

The Socialist International was no more able than the Communists to prevent the outbreak of the Second World War. The
Communist International was formally disbanded in 1943; the
short-lived attempt in 1947 to revive it in the form of the Communist Information Bureau was given up again after a few years.
However, social democracy, after several preparatory conferences,
culminating in a congress in Frankfurt am Main in 1951, again
formed itself into a Socialist International. As the Labor and
Socialist International before it, the Socialist International again
unites nearly all parties that stand by the traditions of social
democracy and the labor movement as much as by the multiparty
system and the rules of an open democracy.[46]

The three-time failure of a social democratic international
exhibits a certain regularity. The First International was torn

apart by struggles over direction, which were organized by theorists of revolution behind whom there was no political power. The Second International proved to be too weak to wrench its member parties from the pull of national solidarity and national chauvinism. The Labor and Socialist International came to an end because it represented in part powerless exiles (from Germany, Italy, the USSR, Spain, and Austria) and in part parties that were entangled in various national coalitions and alliances (the United Kingdom, France, the Scandinavian countries, and the Benelux nations). The International was always pulled back and forth between the two poles of intellectually brilliant but impotent theory and the theoretically modest but at the same time often unprincipled practice.

The example set by the Labor and Socialist International on the eve and at the beginning of the Second World War illustrates this set of problems. The Socialist party of France (SFIO) supported the Munich Agreement, with which the Western powers sacrificed their ally, Czechoslovakia, to National Socialism; the British Labour party opposed this agreement. When German troops invaded Poland, the International's bureau in Brussels had nothing more to remark than that the International was against "a policy of conquest and suppression, and for a lasting peace based on international cooperation and on democratic understanding among the peoples." A clear word of condemnation of National Socialist aggression, as well as a criticism of the Hitler-Stalin Pact, was not possible. Such a position, self-evident for an international social democracy, would have infringed upon the interests of numerous Social Democratic parties, which in some cases as coalition partners adhered to a policy of neutrality. International solidarity was sacrificed to national interests. 47

The Socialist International, revived in 1951, has yet to be subjected to the severe strains entailed by powerless theory and power-entangled practice. However, the parties represented in it have become even more strongly established and stabilized in the 40 years since the collapse of the Labor and Socialist International. The Socialist International is today characterized by parties that are decisive power factors in their countries; they, precisely for that reason, have to take into account the ground rules for gaining and maintaining power in their countries and have to pay for their power with due consideration for national particularities.

TABLE 41: Membership of the Socialist International,
Spring 1981[48]

Country	Full Member
Argentina	Popular Socialist party
Australia	Australian Labor party
Austria	Socialist party
Barbados	Barbados Labour party
Belgium	Socialist party
Canada	New Democratic party
Chile	Radical party
Costa Rica	National Liberation party
Denmark	Social Democratic party
Dominican Republic	Dominican Revolutionary party
Ecuador	Democratic Left party
El Salvador	National Revolutionary Movement
Finland	Social Democratic party
France	Socialist party
Germany (Fed. Rep.)	Social Democratic party
Grenada	New Jewel Movement
Guatemala	Democratic Socialist party
Iceland	Social Democratic party
Ireland	Labour party
Israel	Labour party
Italy	Italian Social Democratic party
Italy	Italian Socialist party
Jamaica	People's National party
Japan	Democratic Socialist party
Japan	Japan Socialist party
Lebanon	Progressive Socialist party
Luxembourg	Luxembourg Socialist Workers' party
Malaysia	Democratic Action party
Malta	Malta Labour party
Mauritius	Mauritius Labour party
Netherlands	Labour party
New Zealand	Labour party
Northern Ireland	Northern Ireland Labour party
Northern Ireland	Social Democratic and Labour party
Norway	Labour party
Paraguay	Revolutionary Febrista party
Portugal	Socialist party
San Marino	Unitary Socialist party
Senegal	Socialist party
Spain	Spanish Socialist Workers' party

(continued)

Table 41 (continued)

Country	Full Member Parties
Sweden	Social Democratic party
Switzerland	Social Democratic party
Turkey	Republican People's party
Upper Volta	Progressive Front of Upper Volta
United Kingdom (Great Britain)	Labour party
United States	Democratic Socialist Organizing Committee
United States	Social Democrats USA

Country	Consultative Parties
Aruba NA	Movimiento Electoral die Pueblo
Curacao NA	Movementu Antiyas Nobo
Cyprus	EDEK Socialist party
Israel	United Workers' party (MAPAM)
Venezuela	Democratic Action (AD)
Venezuela	People's Electoral Movement (MEP)
SUCEE Bulgaria	Social Democratic party+
SUCEE Czechoslovakia	Social Democratic party+
SUCEE Estonia	Socialist party+
SUCEE Hungary	Social Democratic party+
SUCEE Latvia	Social Democratic party+
SUCEE Lithuania	Social Democratic party+
SUCEE Poland	Socialist party+
SUCEE Romania	Social Democratic party+
SUCEE Yugoslavia	Socialist party+

+Party in exile.
Note: SUCEE = Socialist Union of Central-Eastern Europe.

Fraternal Organizations

International Falcon Movement/Socialist Educational International (IFM/SEI)
International Union of Socialist Youth (IUSY)
Socialist International Women

Associated Organizations

Asia-Pacific Socialist Organisation
Confederation of the Socialist Parties of the European Community
International Federation of the Socialist and Democratic Press
Jewish Labor Bund
International Union of Social Democratic Teachers
Labour Sports International
Labour Zionist Movement
Socialist Union of Central-Eastern Europe

The International Arena

The present Socialist International exhibits two features
that distinguish it from the previous Internationals: greater
internationality and a greater involvement in power.

Nearly half of all member parties—20 of 42—come from
outside Europe. Of the parties with consultative status, all
except for the exile parties from Eastern Europe are from outside Europe. The Socialist International of today, at least at
first glance, actually spans the globe; it comprises parties from
all continents.

However, a second look at the member parties shows that
the non-European parties can be divided into three groups:
parties in countries of an Anglo-American character in which
social democracy frequently has a government socialist orientation
(Australia and New Zealand) and only by way of exception has
the status of a minor party (even in the United States, with
two splinter parties); parties in Third World states that allow
social democracy little or no room for action (Argentina, El Sal-
vador, and South Korea); and parties in Third World states
that have a substantial influence on the politics of their countries
(Jamaica, Senegal, and Turkey).

Only the parties of this third group enlarge upon the Eurocentrism of the International. The parties of the first group,
because of their level of economic development and the political
culture of their countries, are European enclaves. The parties
of the second group do, of course, symbolize the international
engagement of social democracy, but they are scarcely determining factors in the International itself.

This de facto Eurocentrism is also reflected in the composition of the Presidium of the Socialist International. The presidents of the International were formerly, without exception,
representatives of European parties, as were the secretary
generals, who direct the International's headquarters in London.
Of the 13 honorary presidents (as of early 1979) 11 come from
European countries. The international claim is reflected only
in the case of the vice-presidents, of whom nine are from non-
European parties, while 10 come from Europe.

Yet, despite this continued key role of European Social
Democracy, one has to speak of a change here. With the re-
constitution of the Socialist International in 1951, only six of
the 34 parties present and fully entitled to vote were non-
European.[50] Of course, the process of internationalization at
work over the nearly three decades since then is in the first
instance only a promise and has not essentially changed the key
role of the parties from Western, Central, and Northern Europe.

TABLE 42: Presidency of the Socialist International, 1979⁴⁹

President
Willy Brandt (Germany)

Honorary Presidents
Trygve Bratteli (Norway)
Walter Bringolf (Switzerland)
Tage Erlander (Sweden)
Jos van Eynde (Belgium)
David Lewis (Canada)
Sicco Mansholt (Netherlands)
Daniel Mayer (France)
Alfred Nau (Germany)
Pietro Nenni (Italy)
Rafael Paasio (Finland)
Bruno Pittermann (Austria)
Giuseppe Saragat (Italy)
Eki Sone (Japan)

Secretary-general
Bernt Carlsson (Sweden)

Vice-presidents
Ichio Asukata (Japan)
Gonzalo Barrios (Venezuela)
Ed Broadbent (Canada)
Bettino Craxi (Italy)
Felipe Gonzáles (Spain)
Bruno Kreisky (Austria)
Michael Manley (Jamaica)
Ian Mikardo (United Kingdom)
Francois Mitterrand (France)
Daniel Oduber (Costa Rica)
Olof Palme (Sweden)
Shimon Peres (Israel)
Irène Petry (Socialist Inter-
  national Women)
Bill Rowling (New Zealand)
Léopold S. Senghor (Senegal)
Mário Soares (Portugal)
Reiulf Steen (Norway)
Anselmo Sule (Chile)
Joop den Uyl (Netherlands)

But the dynamic set in motion by extending to just a few influential parties cannot be fully comprehended by static images of momentary influences. In the foreseeable future scarcely anything is going to change in the Eurocentrism of the International, but the North-South conflict, which is becoming increasingly evident in the International, will determine the future of international social democracy with increasing clarity, either as an overstraining of the contradictions of interest between the established worker's movements of the rich nations and the Social Democratic parties of the poor countries, probably and necessarily leading to a reversion to open Eurocentrism; or in an increasing balance of interests, which would necessarily contribute to the strength of the non-European parties as well as the addition of new parties from the Third World.

The involvement in power of the International's decisive parties signifies both strength and weakness of the organizations at the same time. The fact that many heads of government or opposition leaders belong to the Presidium of the International, as honorary presidents or vice-presidents, adds to the weight of resolutions and actions of the International. The fact that the basis of power for these politicians and their parties lies in electoral success in their own countries and not, say, in recognition at the international level weakens the readiness to make international solidarity a determining factor in one's own action. Social Democratic parties are strong because they are in a position to win national elections; the Socialist International must, therefore, draw its limits where this national interest of the major parties begins.

The International is not an organ that could make decisions that become effective in any directly political way. Here the Socialist International thoroughly resembles the United Nations General Assembly. But like the latter, the International can serve as an important forum for discussion, as a tribune for public resolutions with moral authority, or as an intimate meeting place for important decision makers. The Socialist International is not an independent factor in international politics, but it is an instrument that facilitates the coordination of policy among important parties, especially European parties. That the independent role of the International must not be overestimated is shown by its financial foundation. At the end of the 1970s the budget of the International amounted to approximately half a million dollars yearly. Compared with even a modest commercial enterprise, such a budget is not only downright ridiculous, it also constitutes a mere fraction of the funds established member parties of the International have at their disposal.[51]

The European Arena

The integration of at first six and later nine nations of Europe in the European Economic Community has also induced European Social Democracy to integrate at the European level. Parallel to the founding of the European Economic Community, the Social Democratic parties of the member states entered into consultations on a form of cooperation at the European level. Finally in 1974, the Confederation of Social Democratic Parties of the European Community was founded, with headquarters in Brussels and Luxembourg. This federation joins together the following parties:

Socialist party of Belgium
Social Democratic party of Denmark
Socialist party of France
Social Democratic party of Germany
Labour party of the United Kingdom (Great Britain)

Social Democratic and Labour party of Northern Ireland
Labour party of Ireland
Socialist party of Italy
Social Democratic party of Italy
Socialist Workers' party of Luxembourg
Labor party of the Netherlands

    In the confederation, the Northern Irish Labour party, the Socialist party of Portugal, the Socialist Workers' party of Spain, and the Israeli Labor party have observer status. Observer status is also accorded the Council of Social Democratic Women and the European Young Socialists as well as the European Community's Socialist Teachers Commission.52
    This integration at the European level was motivated by direct election to the EEC's parliamentary assembly. In this European Parliament, which admittedly suffers from a weakness in jurisdiction typical of the beginnings of European parliaments in the nineteenth century, the Social Democratic parties joined together in an independent socialist caucus quite early on. This was the only caucus in the European Parliament in which all nine member states were represented by parliamentarians. Since the right-wing parties were splintered into a Christian Democratic caucus, a Liberal caucus, and a Caucus of European Democrats and Progressives, the Social Democratic caucus was the strongest caucus before the direct election. The first direct election to the European Parliament in June 1979 did, in fact, confirm the Social Democrats as the strongest grouping and as the strongest parliamentary caucus; however, the performance was disappointing. In many countries, such as Denmark and the United Kingdom, the Social Democrats remained below the voting percentages they have regularly come to expect as the minimum in elections to a national parliament.
    This relatively disappointing election result for European Social Democracy is also explained by the fact that many of the Social Democratic parties are skeptical about European unification in the form of the European Communities. The British Labour party in particular, along with the SPD, the largest member party in the group of Social Democratic and Socialist parties in the EC, is swayed by very strong skeptical currents vis-à-vis Europe. This skepticism influenced the turnout of regular Social Democratic voters, who, unlike regular Christian Democratic or Conservative voters, did not go to the polls in their usual numbers. The relatively low voter turnout worked primarily against Social Democracy. European integration is still very much interpreted as a Europe of Christian

TABLE 43: Result of the Direct Election of the European Parliament (Parliamentarian Assembly), June 1979[53]

Percentage of Votes for Member Parties of the Confederation of the Socialist Parties of the EC

	European Parliament	Previous Elections into National Parliaments	Differences
Belgium (BSP/PSB)	23.4	27.4 (1977)	-4.0
Denmark (S)	21.9	37.1 (1977)	-15.2
France (PS)	23.5	24.7 (1978)	-1.2
Germany (SPD)	40.8	42.6 (1976)	-1.8
Ireland (Lab)	14.5	11.4 (1977)	+3.1
Italy (PSI, PSDI)	15.3	13.6 (1979)	+1.7
Luxembourg (POSL)	21.5	29.0 (1974)	-7.5
Netherlands (PvdA)	30.6	33.8 (1977)	-3.2
United Kingdom (Lab)	33.0	37.8 (1979)	-4.8

Members of European Parliament

	1	2	3	4	5	6	7	8
Belgium	7	10	4	—	—	—	3	24
Denmark	3	—	3	3	1	1	5	16
France	22	—	25	—	19	15	—	81
Germany	35	42	4	—	—	—	—	81
Ireland	4	4	—	—	—	5	2	15
Italy	13	30	5	—	24	—	9	81
Luxembourg	1	3	2	—	—	—	—	6
Netherlands	9	10	4	—	—	—	2	25
United Kingdom	18	—	—	60	—	—	3	81
	112	99	47	63	44	21	24	410

Note: 1 = Social Democrats; 2 = Christian Democrats; 3 = Liberals (including French Giscardiens [UDF]); 4 = Conservatives; 5 = Communists; 6 = Progressive Democrats (including French Gaullists [RPR], the Danish Progress party [Glistrup], and the Irish Fianna Fail); 7 = others (Independents, Italian Neofascists [MSI], Danish Antieuropeans, and different regional parties).

Democrats and Conservatives and as the Europe of the founding generation of Konrad Adenauer, Alcide de Gaspari, and Robert Schumann.

The cooperation of Social Democrats in the framework of the EC is by far the most important association at the regional level. The still-present Eurocentric character of social democracy and the mesh of responsibilities in the European Community facilitate and foster a coordination among various Social Democratic parties. Other regional associations are of no importance for social democracy. One example of this is the fate of the Asian Socialist Conference. Brought into existence in Rangoon in 1953, it had to discontinue its activity by 1960.

The Asian Socialist Conference was indeed independent of the Socialist International and yet was closely connected to it through statutes and many parallel memberships. The Asian member parties of the Socialist International were also founding members of the Asian Socialist Conference. Still, the different political conditions confronting Japan's Social Democracy and the Socialist party of Indonesia, for example, as well as the suppression of some member parties by dictatorships (Burma and Vietnam) destroyed the common foundation of these parties.54

The successful cooperation among European parties and the unsuccessful attempts at cooperation among non-European parties are simply a consequence of social democracy's strong bond to Europe. Of course, social democracy is no longer a purely European affair; but it remains primarily a European matter. The proletarians of all nations who are united in the Socialist International, thus in social democracy, are mainly the proletarians of the economically advanced and socially privileged nations. The Social Democratic worker's movement is first and foremost the union of workers who have more to lose than their chains. The Social Democratic worker's movement is, not least because of the successes of Social Democracy, the movement of the comparatively better-off working classes.

FOREIGN POLICY ORIENTATION

Social Democrats played an important part in shaping the foreign policy contours of Europe after 1945. The Socialist International took a position of principled opposition to Communist parties and communist systems, and thus it contributed to East-West polarization in postwar Europe. Social Democratic politicians had key roles in the development of the North Atlantic Treaty Organization (NATO) and in the development of the

European communities. The Belgian Socialist Paul-Henri Spaak, secretary-general of NATO for many years, and the Dutch Social Democrat Sicco Mansholt, long-standing vice-president of the EC's European Commission, are representative of this Social Democratic participation. Social Democracy has played a part in shaping and sustaining military and economic integration of the West in postwar European politics.

Yet, this participation is in no way the general line of European Social Democracy. In the four neutral states of Europe—Switzerland, Austria, Sweden, and Finland—the Social Democratic parties are consistent advocates of neutrality. The Socialist Workers' party of Spain has inscribed the policy of nonalignment on its banner. The skepticism, founded in neutrality, of the Social Democrats of the neutral countries and the skepticism, founded in social policy, of the British Labour party toward the European Community are just as poorly suited to the image of a European Social Democracy working in unity. There were also foreign policy motives that brought about the split in Italian Social Democracy in 1947: the PSDI was Western-oriented, and the PSI initially neutralist. When the Adenauer government set the course for rearmament and Western-oriented alliance politics, the SPD was at first opposed on principle.

Determining Factors of Social Democratic Foreign Policy

The ties with the military and foreign policy bloc of NATO and with the United States are welcomed and affirmed by a majority of the Social Democratic parties of Europe. It is only a minority that objects to such ties for their country and advocates a position of neutrality or nonalignment. But even the basic affirmation of the NATO alliance is not uniformly firm. The Socialist party of France accepts those alliance commitments that accrue to France, but, in complete agreement with the basic lines of Gaullist foreign policy, it opposes any return by France into the integrated command of NATO, out of which DeGaulle had led the country in 1966. The PSI had originally rejected Italy's membership in NATO, and only in the course of the 1950s did it gradually begin to accept this membership as an established fact that could no longer be reasonably reversed. A similarly qualified and skeptical acceptance came from the Socialist party of Portugal, which after the overthrow of the dictatorship had joined in with the general criticism of NATO support for the Salazar and Caetano regimes. The government of Mario Soares had put the country's belonging to the Western defense alliance beyond question, but it made this step clearly in recognition of geopolitical realities and not as a matter of independent preference.[55]

In the second question of decisive importance for the basic foreign policy orientation of Europe, there is likewise a majority position: most Social Democratic parties desired their countries' entry into the European Communities. The parties that are against their nations' membership in the North Atlantic Treaty Organization have in a consistent fashion rejected full membership in the European Communities, which are in many ways involved with NATO. The British Labour party has drawn a qualified middle position; its various tendencies have followed different goals. The overall line of the party was and is that of "Yes, but. . . ." It is the position of a cautious, critical, skeptical "yes" to the United Kingdom's participation in Western European integration.

If one compares the various parties' principal outlooks on NATO and the EC with their respective positions in the spectrum of government socialism and opposition socialism, there is scarcely any connection to be discerned. Both parties with a government socialist orientation (the Social Democrats of Finland, Sweden, Austria, and Switzerland) and a party with an opposition socialist orientation (PSOE) are against NATO membership for their countries. The remaining firmly opposition socialist Social Democracies are positively disposed toward their countries' NATO membership, though with a certain qualified skepticism. The attitude toward membership in the EC apparently does have something to do with government socialism, insofar as it is only government Socialist parties that do not pursue an unequivocal pro EC course, while all opposition Socialist parties and the other government socialists are among the proponents of their countries' involvement in Western European integration.

This connection is not a causal one, however, but accidental. An opposition socialist focal point also means demanding a sharper theoretical demarcation from capitalism and a more resolute struggle against it. The clearly capitalist structures and basic assumptions of the European Communities could in theory be accepted more readily by the pragmatism of the government socialists than by the opposition socialists' emphatic fidelity to principles. The fact that this is not the case in the reality of Social Democracy must stem from causes having nothing to do with opposition socialism and government socialism.

An attempt to establish a connection between government and opposition socialism and foreign policy presents yet another

TABLE 44: Foreign Policy Orientation of Social Democratic Parties

	Degree of Military West Orientation			For or Against EC Membership	
	1	2	3	4	5
Austria (SPÖ)	o	o	Yes	o	Yes
Belgium (BSP/PSB)	Yes	o	o	Yes	o
Denmark (S)	Yes	o	o	Yes	o
Finland (SDP)	o	o	Yes	o	Yes
France (PS)	o	Yes	o	Yes	o
Germany (SPD)	Yes	o	o	Yes	o
Italy (PSI)	o	Yes	o	Yes	o
Italy (PSDI)	Yes	o	o	Yes	o
Netherlands (PvdA)	Yes	o	o	Yes	o
Norway (A)	Yes	o	o	Yes	o
Portugal (PS)	o	Yes	o	Yes	o
Spain (PSOE)	o	o	Yes	Yes	o
Sweden (SAP)	o	o	Yes	o	Yes
Switzerland (SPS)	o	o	Yes	o	Yes
United Kingdom (Lab)	Yes	o	o	Yes	o

Note: 1 = for NATO membership without reservations; 2 = for NATO membership with some reservations; 3 = against NATO membership; 4 = for EC membership; 5 = against EC membership.

This evaluation is based on actual behavior and not on rhetoric; so the British Labour party's position was evaluated in column 4 because Labour cabinets under Harold Wilson and James Callaghan accepted British EC membership despite some anti-EC rhetoric and anti-EC resolutions articulated by Labour party conferences.

paradox: the penetration of the economies of individual countries by foreign capital, thus creating the web of foreign economic relations that is always, at the same time, an economic dependence on foreign interests.

The theoretical position of social democracy is clear in this regard. It criticizes (for example, in resolutions of the Socialist International) the growing influence of multinational corporations, which are indeed the primary vehicles for the penetration of foreign capital into European countries. Thus, for instance, the campaign platform of the Confederation of Social Democratic and Socialist Parties in the European Community, carried on June 6, 1977, states, "The multinational corporations represent

economic powers of an unprecedented magnitude. These multinational enterprises must no longer be allowed to escape the
democratic control of society and the requirements of economic
policy in the individual countries."56

This rather negative attitude on the part of social democracy
toward the growing influence of international capital would lead
one to suppose that in countries in which Social Democrats have
a particularly high power quotient, the influence of multinational
concerns would be relatively small, and that because of this,
a penetration of the economy by foreign capital would likewise
be of little significance. However, a measure of penetration
for gauging economic dependence, covering the beginning and
the end of the 1960s, shows the opposite: The countries with
government Socialist-oriented parties have a much greater
dependence than the countries in which Social Democracy bears
an opposition socialist orientation. The countries often governed
by Social Democrats are much more in the grasp of foreign
capital than those in which Social Democracy has usually been
in opposition or, during that period, illegal (Portugal and Spain).

This at first surprising finding can be somewhat better
accounted for when one notes the rates at which dependence
increased between 1960 and 1968. In the much more dependent
countries of government socialism, the average rate of increase
was much less than in the characteristically opposition socialist
countries. The rate of increase was particularly high in the
two states in which at that time opposition socialism was driven
to extremes, where Social Democracy was able to operate at all
only illegally.

A comparison between the governing power of Social Democracy and foreign involvement in the economy certainly does not
substantiate the notion that Social Democracy is more readily
prepared than other parties to hand over a national economy to
the multinational corporations nor that Social Democracy puts
up less resistance to such a surrender than, say, Conservative
and Christian Democratic or Liberal parties. Rather, one can
assume absolutely no meaningful connection between the penetration of a country by foreign capital and the governing power of
Social Democracy. One should rather assume that various
national factors beyond the question of the party in power are
the determining factors; thus, for instance, the predilection of
Gaullist governments in France for a politics of national autarky
or the inclination of profit-oriented foreign investors (including
multinationals) to invest their capital in countries that are both
socially stable and economically developed. This helps explain
the heavy foreign economic dependence of countries, such as
Belgium, the Netherlands, and Norway.

TABLE 45: Degree of Penetration as an Indicator of Foreign
Economic Dependency[57]

Countries Influenced by Government Socialism

	Degree of Penetration		Power Quotient*
	1960	1968	
Belgium	1.72	2.44	1.3
Denmark	0.39	0.95	2.9
Finland	0.37	1.32	1.6
Germany	0.88	1.09	1.2
Netherlands	2.71	3.26	1.2
Norway	2.35	3.90	3.2
Switzerland	1.73	1.70	1.4
United Kingdom	2.40	2.30	1.9
Average rate	1.57	2.12	

Increase of the average rate: 35 percent

Countries Influenced by Opposition Socialism

	Degree of Penetration		
	1960	1968	
France	0.65	0.56	0.6
Italy	0.52	0.82	0.6
Portugal	0.31	1.14	0.0
Spain	0.20	0.66	0.0
Average rate	0.42		

Increase of the average rate: 90 percent

*See Table 31.

The evidence of foreign dependence, however, shows
primarily that Social Democracy has no effective foreign political
and economic instruments it is able or willing to employ in order
to minimize the penetration of foreign capital. Here it does not
depend directly on Social Democracy at all. Indirectly, however,
Social Democracy can attract foreign capital; when it is invested
with highly developed governing power, in cooperation with a
strong trade union movement, it can guarantee a social peace
secured by a social welfare state. Social democracy as the force
that knows how to most effectively mute the class struggle thus
indirectly creates the general conditions for promising invest-
ments.

In view of such connections, or rather nonconnections,
one is tempted to deny social democratic foreign policy any
independence at all and to classify it as arbitrary foreign policy

of parties without any recognizable, independent character. That would be hasty; it would be a dual simplification. First, social democracy does in fact make certain questions matters of principle even in foreign policy. Thus, in foreign policy Social Democratic parties are both decidedly anticommunist and antifascist. Second, in their foreign policy Social Democratic parties are also national parties.

The ideological dimension of anticommunism and antifascism is found in the theory and practice of social democratic foreign policy. At the height of the Cold War, the Socialist International was a powerful mouthpiece of anticommunism; Social Democratic parties outside the USSR's sphere of influence became avowed enemies of communism abroad. When the Italian PSI abandoned this line, it necessarily resulted in a break with the other Social Democratic parties, a break that could not be healed until 1966, when the PSI (then united with the PSDI) was admitted to the International.58 Social Democratic parties have also been resolutely antifascist; indeed, one can cite their position on the recent fascist systems of Spain and Portugal and the military dictatorship in Greece, more consistently so than Christian Democratic, Conservative, or Liberal parties. Thus, the Socialist International maintained uninterrupted contact with Social Democratic groupings in Spain and Portugal. These Social Democrats, some operating in exile and some in the underground, could then build up a party organization relatively quickly, starting in Portugal in 1974 and in Spain in 1976.59 In this case international solidarity became a foreign policy determinant of European Social Democracy, which worked in both an antifascist and an anticommunist way; it was antifascist because support for illegal Social Democracies was directed squarely against latter-day fascism, and it was anticommunist because the rapid development of Social Democratic parties posed a convincing alternative to equally fast-moving Communists.

Foreign Policy as a Representation of National Interests

Besides the anticommunist and antifascist baseline, another prevailing characteristic of social democratic foreign policy is the commitment to generally or widely accepted national interests. In general, the individual parties of European Social Democracy advocate a foreign policy that corresponds to the main current in their country. The foreign policy of Social Democracy is usually part of a national consensus. Social Democracy has become a national party, national in the sense of a commitment to mainstream conceptions and predominant public opinion.

TABLE 46: Agreement and Disagreement Between Social
Democracy and Mainstream Foreign Policy[60]

Social Democratic and Socialist Parties	Degree of Military West Orientation		For or Against EC Membership	
	Mainstream	Soc. Dem.	Mainstream	Soc. Dem.
Austria (SPÖ)	3	3	3	3
Belgium (BSP/PSB)	1	1	1	1
Denmark (S)	1	1	2	1
Finland (SDP)	3	3	3	3
France (PS)	2	2	1	1
Germany (SPD)	1	1	1	1
Italy (PSI)	1	2	1	1
Italy (PSDI)	1	1	1	1
Netherlands (PvdA)	1	1	1	1
Norway (A)	1	1	3	1
Portugal (PS)	2	2	1	1
Spain (PSOE)	2	3	1	1
Sweden (SAP)	3	3	3	3
Switzerland (SPS)	3	3	3	3
United Kingdom (Lab)	1	1	1	2

Note: 1 = NATO and EC membership without reservations;
2 = differentiated position between; 3 = against NATO and EC
membership without reservations.

This national component to foreign policy of parties that
are formally committed to internationalism provides some explanation for varying foreign policy orientations, as was illustrated
in Table 44. Whether a Social Democratic party is for or against
its country's membership in the North Atlantic Treaty Organization or whether it favors entry into the EC has little or nothing
to do with government socialism or opposition socialism. Setting
such courses is, however, related to the general orientation of
a nation's foreign policy, which is generally the foreign policy
of the relevant Social Democracy as well.

The only clear exception to the otherwise regular agreement between social democracy and national foreign policy is
the stance of the Norwegian Labor party on European integration.
The Norwegian Social Democrats advocated the admission of
their country, as did the Social Democracy of Denmark. Since
this was disputed among the parties and to some extent within
the parties of Norway and Denmark, the question was put to a
referendum. The decision in Denmark was a yes; Norway's

decision was a no. Returning to power in 1973, after the brief interlude of a bourgeois coalition government, the Norwegian Labor party respected the decision from the plebiscite. Despite a theoretical and originally sharp contradiction between the Social Democratic proponents of the EC and the country's ultimate foreign policy against full membership, a de facto harmony has been established. Although governed by Social Democracy, Norway is not a member of the EC; Social Democracy respects this decision, thus, in the end pragmatically putting itself in the mainstream and in the consensus of the country.

In attempting to uncover determining factors behind the foreign policies of individual Social Democratic parties, Werner J. Field has drawn on geography to explain differing conducts.[61] The geographical situation and, inextricably linked with it, an established foreign policy tradition as part of the political culture can best explain the foreign policy of social democracy. The fact that the ideologically consistent anticommunist Social Democracy of Austria endorses its country's policy of neutrality[62] while the Socialist party of France defends its NATO membership, although it had for many years been in an opposition and alternative government alliance with the Communists, can only be explained in geohistorical terms. The neutral and nonaligned nations of Europe have assumed these roles for reasons that can be traced back in every case; those states allied with the United States in the Atlantic alliance likewise have specifically historical reasons for their fundamental Western orientation. These causes, related to the individual state and in that sense national, also determine the foreign policy of social democracy.

The foreign policy of Social Democratic parties is a dependent variable. But in the framework of a general antifascism and an equally general anticommunism, it is not dependent upon an ideological orientation. Western orientation or neutrality (nonalignment) are dependent upon a positional orientation; the history and geography of a specific country determine this position.

Foreign policy is the area in which the Social Democratic parties most strongly agree in principle with other established parties, in particular with the large parties to the right of center. Foreign policy is more clearly consensus oriented than social policy, educational policy, agricultural policy, or fiscal policy. Social Democracy is no longer the party of a principled opposition; it has become an integrated force, an important component of the national consensus. This national role is the critical determining factor of a social democratic foreign policy.

6
Ideology and Party Program

Political Democracy and Economic Collectivism, then,
are the only demands . . . which the Social Democrats are likely to retain if they ever, by a gradual
and peaceful development, acquire the supreme
power. But if they come into power by a sudden
revolution . . . if Social Democrats acquire the
government with all their ideals intact, and without
a previous and gradual training in affairs, then
they may, no doubt, like the Jacobins in France,
make all manner of foolish and disastrous experiments.

Bertrand Russell[1]

Today's social democracy has a long training in affairs
behind it. More than 80 years ago Bertrand Russell considered
two goals of social democracy so abiding and self-evident that
they would survive even the natural refining process that comes
with governing. Today only one of the two goals is self-evident—
political democracy as it is represented by all Social Democratic
parties in theory and in practice. Particularly with the parties
molded by practice in government, economic collectivism has
come to be a social welfarism that has very little to do with the
ideas of the integral Marxist stage.

Social democracy has avoided the "foolish and disastrous
experiments" Russell predicted would follow upon a sudden
coming to power, but at the price of a split and separation from
that part of the European worker's movement that wanted to
establish socialism without political democracy. The warning

against the Jacobin course was taken to heart by that part of the worker's movement that still calls itself social democracy; social democrats have always suffered the Jacobin terror only passively, in some cases from those who also invoke the traditions of the Marxist labor movement.

Yet, political democracy as an enduring, inalienable moral force of social democracy belongs to other currents and other parties, too. Political democracy does indeed distinguish social democracy, but it is not its exclusive property. Social democracy has resisted the temptation of aiming to achieve its human goals by the use of inhuman means. For this very reason, the immediate question is not that of the relationship and cross-ties between social democracy and communism, but rather the following questions, What is the really unique feature of Social Democracy? Does it share the goals and methods of other democratic parties? Does its theory follow from a reality that is hardly distinguishable from the practices of others?

The history of social democracy and the analysis of its present do not support any suspicion of Bolshevism motivated by election tactics or anything else. But they do justify questions as to what distinguishes Social Democracy from the other major people's parties of Europe; whether there really is anything like a specifically social democratic theory, a specifically social democratic program, or a specifically social democratic intellect; and whether a Social Democracy that has become pragmatic and only pragmatic did not long ago sink into the mishmash of catch-all parties in the world's wealthy nations.

PROGRAMMATIC TRADITIONS

Social Democratic parties have always tried to connect their practice with a theory. Bourgeois parties could and can conduct politics without a program; they could and can make do with a few general basic values (such as freedom and performance). No politics is ideology free in the sense of being free of values and interests. But a politics can be theory free in the sense of being free of the connection of political action with a system of values, analyses, and demands.

Of all the party groupings of Europe, Social Democracy is the one that has succumbed least to this temptation to operate without theory. Bourgeois parties conduct politics and in so doing perhaps appeal to great values, which have since tended to become empty slogans. Communist parties have ruled or revolted, but their theory has always all-too quickly smacked of a nimblewitted superstructure thrown up to cover the ruling interests of the USSR. Social Democratic parties, on the other hand, have made programs, and Social Democratic politicians have wound themselves up in heated discussions over fine theoretical points, in the process sometimes missing the point of action or the possibility of governing.[2]

Of course, this has changed. Government Socialist parties know how to take action and how to govern. But the long tradition of party programs and the old respect for theory lives on, at least in remnants and even in those Social Democracies most strongly geared to day-to-day politics.

German Social Democracy has always been considered among the Social Democratic parties that devoted special attention to theory and discussed their programs with a special intensity. The history of German Social Democracy is first of all a history of its programs. In 1875, the first comprehensive program of principles of German Social Democracy was laid down in Gotha, which took place at the same time and place as the unification of the General German Workers' Association, founded by Ferdinand Lasalle, and the Social Democratic Labor party, which was more strongly influenced by Karl Marx. In 1891, a second, new program of principles was adopted by a party conference in Erfurt; once again this theoretical accomplishment paralleled an organizational act. Following the lifting of the antisocialist laws, the party took a new lease on life, naming itself the Social Democratic party of Germany (SPD). Erfurt was considered the theoretical victory of Marxism in social democracy; for several decades the SPD was the central authority for Marxist doctrine and was the leading Marxist party.[3]

Among the parties that were less given to expressing their theory in solemn party programs and their theoretical inclination not so much in the formulation of comprehensive documents was the British Labour party. In British Social Democracy, theory and practice were far less synchronous. When George Bernard Shaw, Sidney and Beatrice Webb, H. G. Wells, and others founded the Fabian Society in 1883, there was still no independent Labour party; but the founding of this society gave rise to perhaps the most important contribution to the theory of British Social Democracy. The Fabians and the other tendencies that, together with the unions and after several attempted starts, finally came to found the Labour party in 1906 were scarcely influenced by Marxism. Their theoretical approach was less that of an all-embracing interpretation of history and society and more that of a moral appeal for the transformation of profoundly unjust conditions.[4]

These two poles are representative of the two methodological traditions in social democracy: socialism as an all-embracing, mainly Marxist-inspired macrotheory attempts to bring all social factors into relation with one another and to explain the ultimate ends of politics, economics, and culture; socialism as a moral protest develops an indignation over the exploitation of man by man into a microtheory of numerous reforms.

These two methodological approaches of social democratic theory are not in opposition but rather are points of emphasis that complement one another. The subsequent development of various aspects of social democratic theory within the different Social Democratic parties was often influenced by both one and then the other approach. Of course, there were also currents in the Labour party that were more strongly bound to Marxist macrotheory, just as obviously there were groupings and positions in Continental Social Democracy that resembled the Fabian model of pragmatic moral microtheory.

The heterogeneity of theoretical variants and party programs in social democracy was held together by a common bond: hostility toward existing political and economic relations, particularly antiabsolutism and anticapitalism. But the remnants of absolutism as a political system were soon swept from the stage of the developed nations of Europe. Capitalism was left. The struggle with capitalism and with what was interpreted as its corollaries—war, nationalism, clericalism—were at the hard core of every formulation of social democratic programs.

This antiposition, which is ultimately always substantiated ethically, this fundamental opposition above all to capitalism was supplemented in the course of the twentieth century by two other oppositions: an opposition to fascism and an opposition to communism.

Anticapitalism, antifascism, and anticommunism are signposts that help locate a continuity, even where national differences and theoretical pragmatism call into question the existence of any sort of theoretical commonality or any kind of social democratic theory.

Bourgeois class society, defined as the division into the propertied and the nonpropertied, is rejected by every kind of social democracy. Whether the alternative is termed the more or less rapid cauterizing of all exploitive relations or their gradual alleviation and ultimate change, capitalism as the embodiment of the status quo has been and is rejected.

The dictatorship of a self-styled, "naturally" superior elite was a malevolent force for social democracy from the start. Political democracy was violated when the reign of terror, in the name of the "Great Leader" and various hollow slogans, got underway first in Italy and then in more and more European states; the much proclaimed "community" finally showed itself to be a cover for nothing but old capitalist exploitation. Social democracy was and is directed in all its theoretical statements against fascism.

The socialism that Vladimir I. Lenin began to construct in Russia was rejected by social democracy—a rejection that necessarily became a defining characteristic, as those social democrats declaring themselves for the October Revolution suddenly were opposed to it. Social democracy criticized and criticizes communism for its leap over historical stages in the Soviet model and the suppression of contending parties and dissenting forces. In its theory, social democracy was and is true to this anticommunism.

This threefold opposition must also include a pro-position. The constructive dimensions of social democratic theory must be concentrated in the areas that Bertrand Russell saw as the enduring elements of social democratic claims: political democracy and a collective economy and, thus, a social democratically inspired political system and a social democratically conceived economic system.

The Political Theory of Social Democracy

The political theory of social democracy was and is that of a political democracy. Social Democratic parties proceed from the assumption that democracy is guaranteed not just by social democracy, but that it can be decisively developed only by it. This insight is the official view of the Socialist International, as expressed at its founding congress in Frankfurt am Main in 1951. "Socialism can be achieved only through democracy; democracy can be fully realized only through socialism."[5]

In Europe the Social Democrats have always constituted parliamentary parties. For them democracy has always been a system whose central point was popular representation according to the principles of universal, free, and equal suffrage. A prime example of this disposition toward parliaments on the part of social democracy is the British Labour party. As the party in power and the majority party in the House of Commons, the Labour party after 1945 eliminated the last remaining privileges of the feudal House of Lords and consummated parliamentary democracy. The Labour party also represents an extreme form of parliamentary intraparty democracy, because it gives the

Lower House caucus a critical function, which is at least equal to the party conference.[6]

But European Social Democrats on the Continent are also well-disposed toward parliament. Swedish Social Democracy, with its absolute majority in the national parliament, put through a constitutional amendment in 1970 that eliminated the last, albeit only, formal vestiges of a constitutional monarchy and installed an ideal type of unicameral parliamentarism. In 1949, in cooperation with Christian Democratic and Liberal parties, the German Social Democrats made a substantial contribution to the realization of the Basic Law, which also bore the features of an ideal type of parliamentary system. The French Socialists had a split position on the constitutional ideas of the Gaullists. A part of the then Socialist party of France (SFIO) became advocates of a parliamentary character to the constitution and were defeated in the referendum; another part of the Social Democrats saw the most important achievements of parliamentarianism preserved in the constitution, which then became the constitution of the Fifth Republic (in so doing they supported DeGaulle on this point).[7]

Everywhere in Europe the Social Democratic parties came out for the free, secret, universal, and equal right to vote. It was the Social Democrats who fought against the feudal Conservative and old Liberal remnants of a restricted suffrage favoring the propertied classes, thoroughly in harmony with their direct party interests. It was also the Social Democrats who unreservedly came out in favor of women's suffrage, not at all in harmony with direct party interests. Equal franchise to include workers was advantageous for the Social Democrats; it strengthened their position in parliament. Women's suffrage had its disadvantages—the tendency toward conservative voting among women weakened the parliamentary position of Social Democracy.

The traditional and the present political theory of social democracy is not, however, exhausted by a perfecting of parliamentarianism. Parliamentarianism as a historical accomplishment, (but not as the ultimate goal for democracy) is the theoretical position that binds the various Social Democratic parties but naturally does not always lead to a consistent or a uniform practice.

One example of these social democratic conceptions of the continued development of parliamentarianism is the historical but also current discussion about elective councils or soviets. It was not just the supporters of the October Revolution but also Social Democrats who in the beginning attempted to erect the experimental Soviet Republics in Bavaria and Hungary. When in the 1960s and 1970s there was a revival of the discussion of soviets, theoretical views were propounded (in the West German Social Democratic party [SPD] for instance) describing certain basic ideas of soviet democracy as thoroughly consistent with social democracy, not as a transcendence of parliamentarianism but as an extension and development of it.[8]

An example of the attempts to carry political democracy further on the ground of parliamentarianism is the theory of self-governing socialism. The concept of a self-governing socialism is put forward above all within the Socialist party of France, which is influenced by the left-Catholic, left-socialist trade union federation Confederation Francaise Démocratique du Travail (CFDT). This is a theory that sees the realization of democracy not only and not primarily by a centralized popular representation but rather by a direct self-determination of individual citizens in their specific spheres of life. Such a democratic theory, tending toward anticentralism and anti-bureaucratism, has attained a great deal of importance mainly for parties with an opposition socialist point of emphasis.[9]

More important than the perfecting of parliamentarianism and the theoretical discussion about soviet democracy and self-government is the stand of social democracy on party pluralism. Independent of the change in concrete social conditions and independent of the heterogeneity of specific national conditions, the affirmation of the multiparty system is the theoretical core of social democracy's political theory. Thus, the Frankfurt declaration reads, "Democracy requires the right of more than one party to exist and the right of opposition."[10] This theory of the multiparty system has also been consistently applied by the Socialist International. Social Democratic parties, unable to come around to a fully unequivocal affirmation of Western democracy, have had to break with the community of the International.

This was an undertaking fraught with conflicts, especially at the height of the Cold War. Parts of Social Democratic parties in Eastern Europe accepted the people's democracy model of a de facto, one-party system, in which Social Democracy and Communism were consolidated under the leadership of Communist functionaries. In 1948 the Social Democratic parties of Bulgaria, Romania, Czechoslovakia, and Hungary were excluded from the International Socialist conference, which was preparing for the revival of the International; these Social Democracies had supported the Communist politics of their countries.[11] The exile parties that were formed subsequent to the Communist development in Europe and that were recognized by the International represented the anticommunist sections of social democracy.

The allegiance to the multiparty system, given a plainly anticommunist interpretation in the period after the Second World War, also led to the exclusion of the Italian Socialist party (PSI). After the split in Italian Social Democracy in 1947, the majority socialists were initially accepted in the International Socialist Conference, despite their continuing alliance with the Communists. However, since the Italian Communists at this time were defending the measures taken by the Communist parties in Eastern Europe, and since the PSI continued to maintain a community of action with the Communists, the PSI was expelled from the International Socialist Conference in 1949. Until 1966 Italy was represented in the International by the smaller Social Democratic party (PSDI); the PSI did not join up with the community of Social Democratic parties until after its break with the Communists and following the reunification with the PSDI (which lasted but three years).[12]

The political theory of social democracy is first and foremost the political theory of Western democracy. Parliamentarianism and the multiparty system are not just conceptions of Social Democracy but also that of the Liberal, Christian Democratic, and Conservative party currents in Europe as well. Social democracy has indeed put these principles into practice with particular consistency. As guardian of this democracy, it has not let itself be outdone in theory and practice by anyone. The special feature of social democratic theory is that it must be reckoned among the staunchest advocates of Western democracy, one of its creators and main defenders.

The special feature of social democratic theory is also that it again and again suggests a sting of dissatisfaction with existing political relations. Soviet democracy and self-government are simply examples of this latent dissatisfaction, formulated primarily by a Social Democracy in opposition. The political theory of social democracy is characterized by a "yes, but . . ." toward the systems in which they can freely develop in Europe and that in some cases they dominate; there is also a clear, unquestionable "yes" to parliamentarianism and the multiparty system but also a recurring desire not to have political democracy end at that.

The Economic Theory of Social Democracy

This sting of theoretical dissatisfaction, which is again and again perceptible in the political theory of social democracy, comes mainly from the realm of economics. The political economy of social democracy is distinguished by greater vagueness, greater noncommitment, and greater dynamics. Bertrand Russell spoke of the collective economy as a residual goal of social democracy; the central theoretical document of modern social democracy—the Frankfurt Declaration—speaks of economic democracy as the essence of all economic goals. "The immediate economic aims of Socialist policy are full employment, higher production, a rising standard of life, social security and a fair distribution of incomes and property."

A similar formulation could come from Christian Democratic parties as well. In view of social democracy's Marxist traditions, the crucial question concerning property relations is answered by the International in a very open-ended, practically evasive fashion. "Socialist planning can avail itself of many different methods. The extent of public ownership and the forms of planning are conditioned by the structure of the individual countries."[13]

Except for the idea of socialist planning, even this formulation could be found in programmatic statements of Christian Democratic parties. Economic collectivism can be and is interpreted quite differently within present-day social democracy; the far-reaching conceptions of socialization, primarily among opposition Socialist parties, and likewise the theoretically formulated break with such conceptions by government Socialist parties are reduced to a common denominator only in a makeshift fashion, with intimations of different conditions in the different countries.

In the area of economics, the tradition of social democratic theory can be traced back with particular clarity to the dependence of theory on practice. Social democracy began as a movement that wanted to change the economic order radically, moving toward a form of collective property that could be conceived of as partly cooperative and partly state-owned. Everywhere that Social Democracy won governing power the practice had to conform with the theory or the theory had to develop further, parallel with the practice.

The economic theory of social democracy was influenced by two types of governing power. Social Democrats in government coalitions with bourgeois parties (Germany after 1918, France after 1936, and so forth), justifiably and judiciously referring to the brakeman function of coalition partners, have not been able to consistently implement their theory. Where the coalition partners were clearly to the right (for instance, in Germany), the stumbling blocks have been greater than where the coalition partners have at times been to the left (as in France). When Social Democrats were the sole party in power, based on a clear majority in parliament (the United Kingdom and various Scandinavian countries since 1945, Austria after 1970), the theory of socializing the means of production had to be confronted directly with a government practice for which only the Social Democrats were responsible.

Social Democrats in government have in fact exerted an influence on property relations (for example, in the United Kingdom between 1945 and 1951), when parts of heavy industry and transportation were transferred into public ownership. Nowhere have the Social Democrats used their power to abolish completely private ownership of the means of production and actually introduce collective ownership, be it only as an overall principle. A Social Democratic government is everywhere characterized by a tolerated, indeed promoted, coexistence of collective and private property; in some states, such as in Scandinavia and in the Federal Republic of Germany, Social Democratic governments or Social Democratic-dominated governments even go hand in hand with a clear priority of private ownership.

The reasons for this adjustment of social democratic theory through social democratic practice are many and varied. The horrible example of communist economic systems, which attempted to apply consistently the principle of collective ownership; the manifold resistance of private industry, which was often successful in influencing the ruling Social Democracy; the concern for economic growth, which would have been threatened by intense conflicts between labor and management—all of these have resulted in the Social Democratic parties of today in no way maintaining the socialization of the means of production as part of its economic theory.

The common denominator of collective ownership has been replaced by the common denominator of economic democracy. Of course, individual Social Democratic parties can imagine quite different things under economic democracy. For the Scandinavian, German, and Austrian Social Democrats, economic democracy means primarily workers participation, represented by the unions, in the central decisions of economic policy and in the direction of business firms, even if the latter remain in private hands. For the Mediterranean Social Democrats this means much more democratizing of the economy from below in the sense of self-governing socialism. The slogan of economic democracy has the advantage of being relatively nonbinding and, hence, of allowing the individual parties a diversity of practice, without their coming into conflict with their theoretical claims in the process.

But the economic democracy formula does describe where the sting of social democratic dissatisfaction sits: in primarily economically determined social inequality, of which political democracy and the most perfect parliamentarianism are capable of changing nothing. However arbitrarily it can be interpreted, the concept of economic democracy implies the minimum postulate of transferring the democratic model onto the economy, and it expresses the idea that the capitalist (that is, unequal) economy should no longer distort without restriction the democratic (that is, equal) polity.[14]

The anticapitalism of social democracy has gone through a change. Even from the point of view of theory, resolute antagonism has been replaced by a modus vivendi tempered by conflict and friction. The Social Democrats have had a hand in changing capitalism; now they no longer confront this altered capitalism with complete hostility but with gradational claims for reform.

The political and economic theory of social democracy is simply the sum of different theories, different philosophies, and different moral conceptions. Social democratic theory reflects the diversity of Social Democratic parties; it is an essentially pluralist theory. It is pluralist in two ways: it is characterized by a horizontal plurality, a coexistence of radical and moderate conceptions of change; and it is marked by a vertical plurality, a hierarchy of scientific social theories, moralizing postulates, and interest-determined demands. In this stratification and, to some extent, inconsistency, the theory and practice of social democracy are one.

CURRENT IDEOLOGICAL DISCUSSION

That mixture of theory, morality, and interest, which is also called ideology, is an important component of everyday political conflicts that Social Democratic parties have to handle. In its everyday function, ideology has an offensive and a defensive function. Ideology is employed offensively when Social Democracy presents its aims and objectives in an optimal way; thus, it disputes the claim of other party ideologies that they serve the good of the community or of a particular group in the best possible way. Ideology is used defensively as Social Democracy counters the attacks of other parties disputing their claim to represent the good of the community or group.

A trademark of any ideological discussion in the multiparty system is the inclination to depict the party philosophy of the other side in the worst possible light and the party philosophy of one's own side in the best possible light. Through this conflict situation of party politics, complicated ideological issues are simplified, and qualified statements are twisted in a propagandistic manner.

One particularly complicated position for social democracy that is repeatedly simplified one way or another in the course of day-to-day political struggles is the relationship between social democracy and religion.[15] In the 1951 Declaration of the Socialist International, meeting in Frankfurt am Main, a formula was developed upon which the various currents and traditions could come to an understanding. This common denominator of a pluralist world view remains today descriptive of the stance of European Social Democracy in its entirety. "Whether Socialists build their faith on Marxist or other methods of analysing society, whether they are inspired by religious or humanitarian principles, they all strive for the same goal: a system of social justice, better living, freedom and world peace."[16]

This open attitude toward any form of religious connection, agnostic independence, or atheistic attitude glosses over the varied traditions, varied analyses, and varied theoretical answers that exist side by side in social democracy today. There is a coexistence of a traditionally Marxist, consciously atheistic, or agnostic current; an anticlerical tradition that, independent of questions of world view or faith, strongly opposes political interconnections with the churches; a liberal openness, which is often indifferent toward existential questions; and a religiously motivated socialism, which has always assumed a minority position within social democracy, primarily in its Protestant or free-church form.

The development of social democracy in the last few decades has entailed a progressive loss of meaning for the atheistic roots, without the significance of the religious-socialist roots having decisively increased in the process. The decline in antireligious or even antichurch antagonisms within social democracy has rather worked to the advantage of the liberal position in social democracy, which is also that of the Frankfurt Declaration and a majority of the programs of Social Democratic parties. Actually, liberal pluralism is the label most often used by Social Democratic people's parties of the cut of Swedish, Austrian, German, or Norwegian Social Democracy. For a government Socialist party, neither a harking back to the atheistic aspects of Marxism nor an official party emphasis on religious socialism would be beneficial. Liberal openness on religious questions follows the trend toward the U.S. catchall party.

TABLE 47: The Overlapping of Basic Ideological Positions
in France[17]

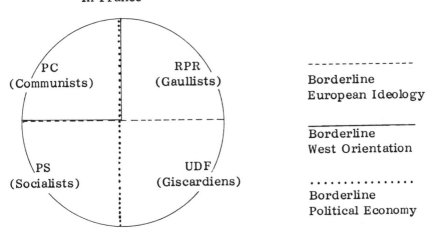

PC
(Communists)

RPR
(Gaullists)

PS
(Socialists)

UDF
(Giscardiens)

- - - - - - - - - - - - - - -
Borderline
European Ideology

———————————
Borderline
West Orientation

· · · · · · · · · · · · · ·
Borderline
Political Economy

Current ideological discussions often pass over the complexity of social democracy's theoretical positions, because the
terms of reference of the theoretical discussions are different.
Thus, to take the example of the Socialist party of France (PS),
on questions of European integration the PS takes roughly the
same theoretical line as the right liberal Union pour la Démocratie
Francaise (UDF) against the skeptical attitude toward Europe
of the Gaullist Rassemblement du Peuple Francais (RPR) and
the Communists. On the other hand, basic doctrine on international politics unites the fundamentally pro-Western parties—
(PS), (RPR), and (UDF)—against the Communist party (PC).
At the level of political-economic theory, however, the PS and
PC occupy roughly one position, that of socializing of the means
of production, while the UDF and RPR maintain the contrary
ideological conception, namely defending private ownership.[18]

The ideological discussion is also encumbered by the
historical change to which individual parties are subject within
the social democratic range. With its ideological point of emphasis, a party may be numbered among the main proponents of a
"right-wing" social democratic position; then in a few years,
on the basis of certain ideological changes, it has to be considered
a part of the left within the Socialist International.

One example of this is German Social Democracy. At the
turn of the century the SPD was considered the most important
guardian of Marxist orthodoxy, a party especially oriented to
principles, with a wealth of theoretical strengths. This ideological assay had already changed by the interwar period, and

since the adoption of the "Godesberg Program" of 1959, the
SPD stands as the paragon of right-wing social democracy.
The elimination of key Marxist concepts from the party program
and the theoretical recognition of important components of the
market economy (and thus, of capitalism) have turned the SPD,
the left-wing headquarters of international social democracy,
into the right-wing party of this very same International.[19]

Social democracy's theory, morality, and catalog of demands
have to be viewed in a threefold span: complexity through ideological diversity within social democracy; complexity through
diversity of outwardly directed ideological antagonisms and
commonalities; and complexity through shifts of ideological
points of emphasis in the course of historical developments.

Every ideological discussion with and about Social Democracy
is a dialogue with a party that is contending with other parties
and other ideologies. The ideological discussion is, therefore,
always related to political direction; it can be led to the right—
to the bourgeois parties and their ideologies—but it can also
be taken to the left—primarily in the direction of communism.
The ideological confrontation with the right serves simultaneously
to demarcate on the left, while the confrontation with the left
demarcates on the right.

Critique from the Right, Demarcation on the Left

With its theoretical roots, social democracy is criticized
from the right. Social democracy is confronted with the claim
that totalitarian, antidemocratic developments are latent in
Marxism or in any form of socialism. The example of communist
systems is attributed not just to Communist parties but to all
currents that derive from Marxism in any form whatsoever and
that are in any way connected with socialism.

One form of this critique takes off on economics. Because
social democracy has in fact virtually accepted certain elements
of the market economy but has never in theory fully affirmed
the liberal free enterprise system, critics already see it traveling
the "road to serfdom."[20] Welfare state actions forced by Social
Democracy in its practice of government thus become—in the
eyes of the critics—preliminary steps in a logical development
toward the perfect planned economy. Sociopolitically motivated
interventions by the state in the economy, the essential instru-
mentality of Social Democracy (but also of other centrist Christian
Democratic parties), are interpreted as a restriction of the freedom of the individual. In this critique, the classic liberal eco-

nomic freedom is an invariable component of an all-encompassing freedom, and restrictions of economic freedom are then directed against freedom in general and against democracy itself.[21]

Another form of this critique takes off with politics. The past and present demarcation between communism and social democracy is qualified and thrown into question as merely a tactical maneuver. "The totalitarian temptation" would apply, according to this critique, not only to all varieties of Communism, including Eurocommunism, but also to Social Democracy, especially when under certain circumstances (as is, in fact, part of the opposition socialist orientation) it seeks arrangements with Communist parties.[22]

Suspicion is cast upon Social Democracy because of its theoretical claim and its ever-recurring programmatic attempts to describe as precisely as possible the development of society and the possibilities for its transformation. A party that calls for intervening in the social fabric is associated by its critics with intolerant, know-it-all thinking and with a lack of historical open-mindedness. Jean François Revel formulates it the following way:

> Everyone makes mistakes. But if to err is human,
> it would seem dangerous to entrust power to those
> who consider themselves exempt from that rule and
> are convinced they have never blundered either in
> conception or execution. Before, during and after
> the disasters they inflict on others and themselves,
> it is their invariable custom to attribute exclusively
> to fascist and capitalist machinations the warnings
> they receive, the objections that are raised and the
> accounting that is demanded of them.[23]

The critique from the right pushes social democracy in the vicinity of communism. Hence, this critique provokes a demarcating of social democracy on the left. Social Democracy feels challenged to stress the theoretical dividing line separating it from Communist parties.

This demarcation on the left often goes hand in hand with a social democratic critique of Marxism. This "right-wing" theory sees social democracy as no longer the sole legitimate heir of Marxism but as a unity to be delineated in theory and practice from Marxism. In this view, Social Democratic parties no longer have to contend with Communist parties for the right of succession to Karl Marx; rather, they ought to leave this title safely to the communists. In the eyes of this right-wing social democracy, Lenin is anything but the violator of Marxism but is rather its executor. Alexander and Gesine Schwann, in their argument with "left-wing" social democracy, lay on the communists' doorstep the right to call themselves Marxist in order to excommunicate Marxist social democrats.

> Leninism represents the way and form in which
> Marxist theory has attained that political-practical
> effectiveness which is the main reason it is again
> and again taken seriously—precisely as theory, as
> a theory of practice—although it represents in
> many respects an antiquated product of the 19th
> century. Marxism and Leninism, Marxist theory
> of practice and Leninist theory of practice—in
> historical, theoretical and political terms they are
> not to be abstracted from one another.[24]

The critique from the right has thus become an element of the intraparty ideological debate of Social Democracy itself. Marxism and the central concepts of Marxian analysis of society furnish the buzz words at which the argument rises up. Whether the Social Democratic parties represent the genuine practice of Marxist theory; whether the Social Democratic parties are theoretically so pluralistic as to permit Marxist theory, too; or whether Social Democracy and Marxism are mutually exclusive—all that has in fact been answered long ago in the practice of all Social Democratic parties in favor of the middle, open, pluralist position. But theory is the level from which these standpoints continue to clash with one other. Thus, Rudolf Wohlgenannt makes use of the theory of social democracy or democratic socialism, which he sets in opposition to Marxism. To the Marxist conception ("the classless society is in principle possible") he counterposes the social democratic theory. "The classless society is indeed desirable, and Democratic Socialism does strive for it. But Social Democracy is more skeptical than Marxism. The struggle against class domination is viewed as a permanent duty because these sorts of positions and tendencies can arise again and again, in any social system and for any number of reasons."[25]
    Thus, there is a broad range of criticism from the right. It extends from sharply anti-social democratic attacks to positions within social democracy; it comprises the reproach that social democracy is latently totalitarian because it is Marxist, as well as the claim that social democracy was not Marxist precisely because it was not totalitarian. The critique always centers

on Marxism, which is either attributed to social democracy or renounced by social democracy once and for all.[26]

Still, this range is evident not only in the case of right-wing criticism; it applies as well to criticism from the left. Here, too, positions range from expressly anti-social democratic to explicitly social democratic; here, too, Marxism and its central concepts furnish the critical buzz words. Of course, the directional pull is precisely the opposite; the critique from outside reproaches social democracy with a betrayal of Marxism; the critique from within claims Marxism for social democracy. The interpretation of Marxism is the key to understanding social democracy and the individual social democratic currents.

Critique from the Left, Demarcation on the Right

Because of its pragmatic inclinations, Social Democracy is criticized from the left. The criticism is that Social Democrats have cut themselves off from their ideological roots and that they have betrayed the theory with which they had once set forth to transform society.

Social democracy as an agent of advanced capitalism and an instrument that yields the loyalty of the workers for a system of worker exploitation—this is the constantly recurring reproach in a number of variants of a theory that focuses Marxism primarily on property relations with respect to the means of production. "In this way 'democratic socialism' proves to be a new edition of 'perfected' capitalism."[27]

The critique comes not only from Marxist-Leninist theorists of the orthodox faith, who are committed to the Soviet model of society. It comes from Eurocommunists and left socialists as well. Santiago Carrillo takes pains to delineate his design as clearly as possible from that of Social Democracy.

> On the other hand, there cannot be any confusion between "Eurocommunism" and social democracy in the ideological sphere, not at least with social democracy as it has manifested itself up to now. What is commonly called "Eurocommunism" proposes to transform capitalist society, not to administer it; to work out a socialist alternative to the system of state monopoly capitalism, not to integrate in it and become one of its governmental variants.[28]

This left-wing critique from without sees in Social Democratic practice only cosmetics on the system, a mere altering of

the image of the society, while the exploitative capitalist character remains unchanged. Social Democracy is the one that
arranges this specially refined sales technique. For its services,
according to this critique, it is involved in ruling and adminis-
tering the existing system of injustice. "Assimilation into
ruling power is the reward for renouncing opposition."29

The thrust of this criticism does not pertain to the theoretical claim of social democracy but rather to the lack of practical
application of this theory. This critique, formulated as empirical
findings, extends deep into social democracy; it is formulated
by disillusioned socialists outside Social Democracy, but also
by those still within Social Democratic parties. Ralph Miliband
criticizes British Social Democracy, saying the following:

> The Labour Party is no longer even a "reformist"
> party. "Reformist" socialism is the belief that a
> socialist society will be brought into being by way
> of a gradual series of structural and social
> reforms. . . . The leaders of the Labour Party
> have no such strategy and, except for merely
> rhetorical purposes, want none of it. They may
> occasionally prattle on about socialism, but this,
> on any serious view of the matter, lacks all effec-
> tive meaning. 30

The absence of a strategy that transforms theory into
practice and brings closer the goal of a socialist and democratic
society is also the complaint of socialist theorists within Social
Democracy. Not so much the What as the How motivates left-
wing critics who regard their own theoretical position as social
democratic or democratic socialist. It is government socialism—
which not only discusses social democracy but tangibly carries
it out as well—that is the cause and object of this critique.
"The central problem for a strategy of democratic socialist
reforms . . . lies in the development of a realizable Social
Democratic economic and social policy."31 That is how Peter
von Oertzen put it after many years of high-level involvement
in the Social Democratic government in the Federal Republic of
Germany; this critique ultimately criticizes Social Democracy
for policy that is not social democratic: it is just a policy like
any other, something the bourgeois parties could do.

This skeptical view of the practice of Social Democracy on
the part of Social Democratic theorists leads to a theoretical
demarcation vis-à-vis traditional practices of Social Democracy.
The object of this critique is linear and quantitative growth-

oriented thinking, a distribution policy understood in sheer
material terms, the equation of security and prosperity with
socialism. This Social Democratic skepticism toward parts of
the Social Democratic tradition is tied to a general skepticism
about the ideology of growth, about the simple extrapolation
of previous policy. Awareness about the menacing ecological
crisis is linked with the Marxist claim of changing society.
Criticism of centralism and bureaucratism even of the social
welfare state created by Social Democracy are concrete forms
of this theory of a Social Democratic "left center." Egon Matzner,
who does not see the welfare state as the ultimate goal of democratic socialism, formulates this critique in the following terms:

> Even if, compared to the liberal watchdog state,
> there is a glimpse of strong social progress favor-
> ing mainly the socially weaker elements, for social-
> ists there exists no apparent reason to see the goal
> of their political efforts in bureaucratized bourgeois
> society. For bureaucratic domination and public
> assistance are opposed to egalitarian democratic
> principles. [32]

This internal critique does not comprehend socialist theory
as an exegesis of the holy books of classical Marxism, as do
orthodox communist authors. But it sees itself in a tradition
of Marxism; it seeks to continue its development. If Marxism
is rejected by the right wing of Social Democracy, then it is
carried on and adapted by the left wing. If the right wing
defends the existing accomplishments of Social Democracy in
the form of the social welfare state, then the left wing regards
these accomplishments essentially as prerequisites for Social
Democratic social policy but not yet as its results.
　　Today Social Democracy has learned to live with these
tensions and contradictions. It has its wings, as do bourgeois
parties. Social Democracy's inclination toward more theory is
expressed in a more intense theoretical discussion between
these wings. Thus, Social Democracy is no more torn with
dissension than other major parties and major currents; yet,
it is anything but the representative of a unified theory.
　　In view of its internal ideological range and in view of
the criticism brought against it from the far left and likewise
from the right, Social Democracy makes do with a pragmatic
theoretical pluralism. The Social Democratic center is in fact
underrepresented in the discussion of ideology and theory;
but it does furnish the critical formulations for securing Social

TABLE 48: Critique On and Inside Social Democracy

Reproach: SD is Marxist	Claim: SD is not Marxist	SD is Marxist and not Marxist	Claim: SD is Marxist	Reproach: SD is not Marxist
Ideologies right of SD	Right wing	Center Ideological positions inside SD	Left wing	Ideologies left of SD
Analysis: Western industrialized society is not an exploiting society anymore		Analysis: Stage between to be improved by SD	Analysis: Western industrialized society is still an exploiting society	
in spite of SD	because of SD		in spite of SD	because of SD

| CRITIQUE FROM THE RIGHT | DEMAR-CATION TO THE LEFT | | DEMAR-CATION TO THE RIGHT | CRITIQUE FROM THE LEFT |

Democracy's organizational unity, despite ideological diversity.
This center, committed to Social Democratic pluralism, is prepared in principle to accept all currents not expressly directed
against the party and its interests in power, not expressly
violating the taboo of anticommunism and antifascism, and not
expressly seeking a consonance with bourgeois parties. As
long as the practice is not threatened, freedom through diversity
prevails in the theory. 33

RELATION OF THEORY AND PRACTICE

Social democracy is no school of philosophers. The striving
not merely to interpret the world but to change it extends from
Karl Marx to the government socialism of the present. Theory
as an end in itself was and is alien to social democracy.
Theory has a purposive function in social democracy. It
can and should describe the contours of the societies in which
Social Democratic parties are established. It can and should
formulate the principles that social democracy has to follow. It
can and should help create consciousness, in order to make
Social Democratic politics possible.

One example of this form of theory working in practice is the Report of the Working Group on Questions of Equality of the Social Democratic Workers' party of Sweden and of the Swedish Trade Union Federation, a report prepared under the chairmanship of Alva Myrdal and presented to the public in 1969. This program of Swedish Social Democracy dispensed with any comprehensive philosophy of history and any attempted clarification of existential and eschatological questions. It summarized all the values that have importance for social democracy under the central value of equality. It determined that there was a "need for equality" and that equality had not been realized; it developed a comprehensive program of action for establishing more equality. "Social Democracy has given substance to the idea of equality, namely that all men are equally entitled to lead a life of promise and fulfillment."[34]

This conclusion is neither theistically nor atheistically substantiated. But it is the pivotal point for a far-reaching and, in the end, radical reform project—for a fundamental transformation of society by means of a many-sided strategy extending from wage policy to educational policy to judicial policy.

This form of social democratic theory aims quite openly at practice. But it is no simple vindication of Social Democratic action. A Social Democracy, such as the Swedish Social Democratic Workers party (SAP), which sets for itself a radical reform program after decades of government activity, is indirectly admitting that its own policy in the past was perhaps good but inadequate and that a Social Democratic government in no way signifies a Social Democratic society already exists.

Such a theory for practice cannot claim to be a macrotheory that explains all that is social and all that is human. It is not, however, simple political know-how nor just technocratic political specifications, severed from the questions concerning the meaning and purpose of influence and power.

Practice influences theory by conveying the ground rules of democracy. In order to make theory real and be able to transform society according to the goals of social democracy, a Social Democratic party must first of all win elections, and to do so it needs the support of a majority of the population. Social democracy as a program without a majority is a theory remote from practice—in this sense an unreal theory. Hence, a party cannot allow itself to formulate its theory exclusively according to criteria of analytic acuity, methodological cogency, and strict fidelity to principle. Its exclusive concern cannot be standing for truths or socialist correctness. It must also and first of all be sure that it can communicate its supply of truth, reach its constituents with its ideology, and gain the support of a majority of the voters.

This is the consequence of such democratic ground rules: the ideology is not the better one that can prove to itself the greatest degree of scientific foundation or cogency but rather the one that knows how to mobilize majorities in its interest. In democracy it is not some sort of quality—undemonstrable anyway—that legitimizes but rather a quantity of consent from below.

Thus, any party, but especially one with a rich tradition of theory, like a Social Democracy, gets into a bind of deideologization. It must offer its store of socialism measured out in doses in order to be able to gain a majority. It must not present the full abundance of its theory; rather it must calculate exactly how much socialism can really be expected of the voters that are necessary for winning a majority. Precisely because social democracy is democratic, there exists an iron law of reduction in socialism. Socialism is chopped up into salubrious portions and indigestible parts are left out.

The bind of deideologization and the iron law of reduction of socialism are, of course, not statically but dynamically effective. They apply under various social conditions in various ways. In the store of socialist ideas, what is still unreasonable today can well be quite reasonable tomorrow, or in five years, or in ten years, because it sustains a majority; what is still a majority-sustaining ideology today can tomorrow go beyond what can be expected and beyond that which is reasonable for social democracy.

As pertains to the bind of deideologization, in order to be able to put into effect parts of its goals, social democracy must dilute and at the same time enrich its theory. It has to leave out everything that, according to the most precise possible analyses (primarily with the aid of opinion polling) does not appear acceptable to critical borderline and floating-voter strata. Ideological elements must be incorporated into the image of social democracy, which has nothing to do with the original moral thrust and theory.

As pertains to the law of reduction in socialism, the falling by the wayside of theoretical elements applies above all to the central stock of socialist tradition. Essential parts, which in the integral Marxist stage were self-evident and inalienable, are sacrificed in the pluralist post-Marxist stage, pushed to the margins, and turned into an obsolete tradition. The socialization of the means of production is no longer capable of sustaining a majority, hence it is shunted into the museum of the worker's movement. Philosophical materialism ruffles all too many feathers of all too many voter groups, hence it is banned to a siding, where social democracy has, for equally valid reasons, also set aside the dictatorship of the proletariat and the socialist revolution.

Social democracy can no longer ask, Which interpretation of socialism benefits a given society? Rather it must ask, How much socialism can we allow ourselves in order to be able to come to the levers of central political control? The formula is not how much socialism is necessary, but how much is possible.

In a system of competitive democracy, Social Democracy must pay heed to its competitors. Even its theory is related to competition; it must win over the marginal voters, those swing voters who are just as open to the rival parties, for it needs more than its fully convinced regular voters to gain a majority. It must sacrifice parts of its "pure" doctrine and precisely those parts that are specifically socialist, form part of the specific consciousness of core strata, or, for that very reason, cannot make Social Democracy acceptable beyond the hard-core minority.

In order to be able to win over voters, Social Democracy must water down its theory; it has to sacrifice parts of its socialist conviction. This often leads to a confrontation, with the reproach that Social Democrats are moral traitors, and that they are—almost from a defect of character—opportunistic. This moralizing, which comes precisely from the left and as such has little to do with Marxism, utterly fails to come to grips with reality. Social democracy comes under the constraints of deideologization and the reduction of socialism, because it is true to principle, and, unlike communism, it does not sacrifice the principle of democracy or the theory of socialism.

Social democratic theory means that democracy takes precedence over socialism. Socialism is fine, but only if it can be achieved democratically. This fidelity to principle binds social democracy into the ruling consciousness, which is determined as well by nonsocialist and by antisocialist interests. It sets forth into the arena of competitive democracy, because it cannot and does not want to force the felicity of socialism on a reluctant majority. It submits to a reduction of socialism, because it submits to the ground rules of the democratic multiparty system; it is first and foremost democratic.

To criticize social democracy for this accommodation to the prevailing subjective conditions means wanting to replace political strategy with moral pathos or wanting to disregard the principle

TABLE 49: Bind of Deideologization, Law of Reduction
in Socialism[35]

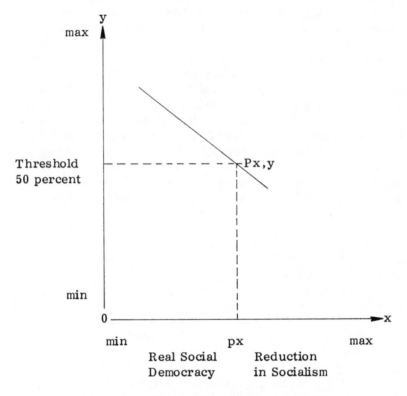

Px,y = degree of socialism articulated by a Social Democratic
party without jeopardizing the majority
x max-px = degree of the reduction in socialism—this part of
ideology that has to be victimized for the (rational) deideologization
x = degree of socialist purity in theory and practice represented by a Social Democratic party
y = degree of agreement (in percent of votes) that can be
gained by specific policies of a Social Democratic party

of Western democracy, which is competitive democracy. Social democracy can in no way be censured for this, for it has, at least since its severance from the Leninist variety of Marxism, emphasized the primacy of democracy and always sought to realize socialism in harmony with democracy.

Social Democracy can only be criticized with not having or having too little utilized the opportunity to change the existing consciousness in a concerted manner. Democratic ground rules include a respect for the majority consciousness, but they do indeed allow for acting upon this majority opinion and wanting to alter it gradually. The criticism of Social Democracy is that because of its practice it forgets theory altogether; it does not use its possibilities as government socialism to change the consciousness of today in the direction of another consciousness for tomorrow, with a minimum of change today to stir a readiness for greater changes tomorrow.

In its theory social democracy is firmly bound to its practice; there is no getting out of the bind of deideologization and the law of the reduction of socialism. What it can do is to reduce gradually the hold of that bind and diminish the extent of the reduction in socialist theory. It can let the dynamic of democracy work for it. If it does this, then it cannot really be criticized for the practice orientation of its theory; but if it forgets about this, then the criticisms touch home.

Theory from Practice: The Case of Religion

The elasticity of social democratic theory has its limits. The most important taboo that social democracy can be shown not to have violated is political democracy. Not only in practice but also in theory Social Democracy has never justified the suppression of rivals as they themselves stand upon the grounds of democracy.

However, in the framework of widely set bounds, social democratic theory is very elastic. One area in which this flexibility of theory is especially clear is in the position of social democracy to religion and the church. In this context social democracy has to proceed from wide national variations—from countries with a strongly Catholic character to traditionally Protestant countries and societies of a mixed denominational structure. However, the direction of social democratic theory in the twentieth century is unmistakable; it is clearly moving away from antireligious and antiecclesiastical positions.

French socialism offers one example of this. Jean Jaures, who represented Franch socialism in the years prior to the First World War, formulated its theoretical position in the following terms in 1899: "Even if the idea of God were to assume a tangible form, if God himself were to arise visibly over the masses, the first duty of man would be to deny obedience and to treat Him as an equal with whom one discusses."[36]

This antitheist conception, which has to be understood in the specific French context of the conflict between church and state, was gradually changed. The left Socialist party, Parti Socialiste Unifié (PSU), which was founded in 1958 and which over a decade later was partially incorporated into the newly formed Socialist party of France, united Socialist and left-wing Catholic positions. Since 1968, the originally Catholic trade union CFDT has been moving closer to the Socialists.[37] The theoretical stance of the Socialist party of France has also undergone a fundamental change; in accord with the Declaration of the Socialist International of 1951, it is open toward any form of religious motivation to socialism. In its statements of principle, it is no longer anticlerical or antiecclesiastical, but rather takes a pluralist position on world views and is tolerant toward the social position of the church.

A similar development can be observed in Austrian Social Democracy. In its Austro-Marxist stage, social democracy had drawn an admittedly not antireligious, yet anti-clerical position, receptive to the Marxist critique of religion. At that time, between the world wars, it stood in sharp opposition to the alliance of church and state conveyed by political Catholicism. After 1945 this antagonism was defused in Austria. Social democracy has gradually changed its theoretical position. In 1958, it adopted, in parts verbatim, the Frankfurt Declaration of the International, and in its party program of 1978, the Austrian Socialist party (SPÖ) official party policy read, "Today millions of Christians are in the socialist movement because they are convinced that in it they can most effectively stand up for their basic ethical values. They are socialists not although, but because they are Christians."[38]

This change does not signify any conversion to Christianity on the part of social democracy. Nor is it motivated by a naked opportunism. Rather it reflects a historical learning process. The iron law of reduction in socialism has had its effect in this context. For the integral Marxist social democracy around 1900, religion was an instrument of the ruling class, used for diverting the feelings of those deprived of their rights from the here and now to the beyond. This at least antichurch but ultimately antireligious position of principle was a natural component of social democracy's conception of socialism. Since then social democracy has learned and processed in its theory that religion is more than an opiate of the people administered to the ruled by the rulers, and that it is rather a need that survives changes in class relations; that national variations pose various strategic problems for Social Democracy, but that Social Democracy is not capable of sustaining a majority anywhere with an unequivocal antichurch position of principle; and that philosophical consistency is in the long run not to be sustained in a secularized environment, rather Social Democracy must accommodate itself to the general plurality in order to survive as a leading democratic party in this environment.

This motif of change has been complemented as well by a parallel capacity for change on the part of the Christian churches, which have loosened up or even given up their alliances with conservative forces and have opened up toward many socialist views in their social doctrines.

This reciprocal change has not been capable of altering the fact that the basic electorate and membership of Social Democratic parties in Europe continues to maintain a certain distance from the core strata of the Christian churches and that the intensely involved milieus of church and social democracy overlap only by way of exception. This reciprocal change has, however, also resulted in a substantial part of the antagonisms that marked the beginning of the twentieth century having disappeared by the end of this century.

Of course, theory did not directly effect this change; rather, theory is the result of practice and the product of interest—both of Social Democracy and of the churches.[39] From its insights into social and political realities, social democracy has in some respects shifted its theory; it has achieved success in its practice with this partially altered theory. Social democracy theory is no article of faith from which it seeks to forcibly master social practice. Theory is much more the abstraction of its political interest in being socially effective.

Theory from Practice: The Case of Communism

A similar law of movement of social democratic theory can be seen in the case of its relationship to communism. Two of the defining characteristics of Social Democratic parties are their rejection of the idea of a socialist revolution in a country that has not yet been industrialized and their opposition to any

form of one-party system, even if this system cites Karl Marx
as authority. Because of this fundamental dissent on questions
of democracy, there can be no complete agreement between social
democracy and communism.

However, this fixed boundary line does allow for differing
theoretical statements on the value of communism and Communist
parties. Social democracy can define communism as a main
enemy, which, like fascism, is to be opposed unconditionally
and with which there can be no theoretical or strategic commonality; or as a rival from whom one is divided by numerous contradictions (but still just one rival among many) and a competitor
with whom, therefore, there can indeed be planes of agreement,
particularly in the rivalry with bourgeois parties and ideologies.

The first position of principle is essentially that of government socialism, the second that of opposition socialism. Government socialism characteristically entails a connection between
its own relatively high power quotient and a relative weakness
of the opposing Communist party (with the exception of Finland);
opposition socialism's relatively low power quotient is accompanied
by a relatively strong Communism. Hence, government socialism
has really no serious competition from the left, does not really
need to fear the Communist parties, and can essentially concentrate on the competition from the right. Opposition socialism,
on the other hand, does have serious competition from the Communist parties, which do indeed press them hard.

In the multiparty system, competition does not mean
mutual repulsion but mutual attraction. Convergence through
competition—this is expressed structurally and theoretically
as well. In order to be able to reach certain strata of the
electorate in the interest of electoral success, an opposition
Socialist party has to make statements that speak to the border
line voters on the left. In this way opposition Socialist parties
face strong pulls straining theoretical consistency; they must
argue to the left and to the right. Government Socialist parties
(again, with the exception of Finland) are spared this; they
can concentrate on right-wing competition, as theoretically
they must make an opening only to the right.

It has been opposition Socialist parties that in the framework of the Socialist International have somewhat restrained
absolute, unqualified anticommunism. In 1972 the International
gave theoretical formulation to what many of its member parties
had already been practicing: the possibility of tactical collabora-
tion with Communist parties. First, there was the practical
situation of competition; then followed the theory of the International. [40]

TABLE 50: Strategic Competition of Government Socialism
and Opposition Socialism

Conservative, Christian Democratic, Liberal parties	Social Democracy	Communist parties (unimportant)

Competition for Government Socialism (exception: Finland)

Conservative, Christian Democratic, Liberal parties	Social Democracy	Communist parties

Competition for Opposition Socialism

However, government Socialist parties as a rule insist on
strict anticommunism. Thus, in its Godesberg Program of 1959,
German Social Democracy stressed, "The Communists wrongly
appeal to socialist traditions. In reality they have falsified the
store of socialist ideas. Socialists want to realize freedom and
justice, while Communists exploit society's internal strife in
order to establish the dictatorship of their party."[41]
    German Social Democracy, an example of a government
Socialist-oriented party, continues to hold steadfastly to this
unqualified condemnation, which permits no tactical exception.
It uses this programmatic fixation in order to settle intraparty
conflicts, but it also utilizes this stipulation to underscore its
credibility on the right and remove any suspicion of proximity
to communism.
    This anticommunist rigidity comes easily to the SPD; it
has nothing to win on the left but much to lose on the right.
This same rigidity in the case of the Socialist party of France
or the Socialist party of Italy is hardly reasonable. The consequence is not just differing strategies, which at times result in
opposition alliances between Social Democracy and Communism
in the Mediterranean countries; the consequence is also a differently accentuated theory. The most important example of this
opposition socialist turn from a priori hostile confrontation with
Communism is the common alternative program for government
signed in France in 1972 by Socialists, Communists, and left
Liberals.[42]
    This alliance with the Communists, of course, also helped
make possible the upswing of the French Socialist party, which
came primarily at the cost of the Communists. The French

development, which led to Mitterrand's victory in the presidential elections and, following this, to the Socialist party's success in the 1981 parliamentary elections, represents a unique case in the history of Social Democracy. Through its alliance with the Communists, Social Democracy won on the left—at the expense of the Communist party—while at the same time, despite its alliance with the Communists, it won in the political center—at the expense of the bourgeois parties.

These differences in theory do not mean that Social Democracy has no principles vis-à-vis Communism. Yet, the differences do permit the conclusion that, given unqualified fidelity to political democracy, Social Democracy attempts to structure its relationship to Communism according to the existing situation. So long as the Communist parties have not broken their close affinity for the dictatorship of one-party systems under a Communist signature, then the borders between Social Democracy and Communism are not fluid. However, under certain conditions, Social Democracy is prepared to form limited alliances with Communists, and hence it is prepared to justify these alliances theoretically.

The relation between social democratic theory and social democratic practice is neither an idealistic nor a simply opportunistic one. Most assuredly, social democracy does not direct its political action according to laws (in the form of theoretical postulates) it has laid down as eternal truths. But precisely because of its theoretical traditions and its constant interest in theoretical questions, social democracy is not in the position of quickly cutting a passing theory to fit particular, often changing tactics. That stands contrary to the consciousness of tradition among social democracy's adherents and to the efforts to establish credibility among marginal voters. Rather, theory and practice are linked with one another in a very complicated way; they determine one another. Social Democracy needs a theory to justify itself within and without. It needs a theory that is not all too far removed from practice. Even if, in view of the diversity of Social Democratic politics, these last limits of theory and of practice are drawn very broadly, they give the surety that Social Democratic politics are not completely arbitrary and that not anything and everything can be sold under the label of social democracy. Total arbitrariness of theory would contradict Social Democratic practice, which is in fact democratic.

Social democratic theory is indeed a product of Social Democratic practice, but it develops a life of its own, which in turn reacts upon practice. However much theory may be engendered for tactical and short-term reasons, it does hinder

precipitous changes by setting fixed standards by which practice
can be gauged. That is the one difference, explicable by the
nature of parties themselves, between European Social Democracy
and the Democratic party of the United States. In social structure and in practical political workings, U.S. Democrats are
fully comparable to a government socialist-oriented Social Democracy. However, the Democrats lack the theoretical tradition
and the standard and corrective that comes out of practice but
in turn influences practice. [43]

7

The Future of
Social Democracy

History consists of necessary accidents.

Hermann Broch[1]

From its history and for its future, social democracy has
a neither-nor to learn: it can shape the future neither by
naively, idealistically wanting to force its humanitarian aims
and objectives onto reality nor by simply relying on the course
of history and wanting to be the mere executor of objective
necessity. But from the successes and failures of its past and
present, social democracy has also come by an equally dialectical
both-and for the future: Abstaining from power in itself means
nothing, just as possessing power in itself is meaningless.
Social democracy has to want power, but at the same time it
must be prepared to give it up again; it must not seek power
for the sake of power, but it must also not shun power from
the start.

Social democracy is not faced with the problem of profess-
ing either a vulgar materialism or a vulgar idealism. Social
democracy is confronted with a vulgar materialist temptation,
which is camouflaged in a vulgar idealist array. The vulgar
materialist temptation is characterized by an abandonment of
any transformation of society, while concentrating on the sheer
administration of society; an increased capability for sustaining
a majority and thus gaining a ruling majority by means of a
complete identification with existing conditions; and a reaction
to social changes instead of a direction for the social future.
On the other hand, the vulgar idealist camouflage is characterized by a formulation of beautiful goals without an analysis of

one's own reality; an intense ideological debate without reference to one's own practice, especially to one's action in government; and socialism as an opiate to conceal nonsocialist reality.

If Social Democracy gives in to this temptation, then it becomes interchangeable, a party like all the rest, though of course a party with a fraudulent label. It becomes a driven force, though it calls itself a driving force; it is merely a product of its environment, though it fosters the illusion that it would shape that environment.

Social democracy—driving force or driven? This is the question of Social Democratic parties' integration into the existing political and social reality. That Social Democracy is largely integrated and that it ought to be largely integrated in order to be capable of establishing a majority and governing is a consequence of its practice-oriented claim to change. That Social Democracy can be completely integrated is a possible consequence of a reconciliation with social conditions.

Social Democracy has changed these social conditions precisely where it shows a government socialist profile. But nowhere has this gone so far that in the prevailing self-image this could be construed as the end point of Social Democracy's will to change. A reconciliation with the society in which Social Democracy operates and which it has already influenced would run counter to all claims. If Social Democracy gives up all distance to existing relations, then there remains no substance, only a name, even if parties determine politics under its name.

The theory and practice of European Social Democracy in no way justify the suspicion of Bolshevism, which for tactical reasons is again and again brought up against it. The theory and even more so the practice of Social Democracy do, however, justify the suspicion of hedonism.

Social Democracy has to face squarely the notion that it is concentrating its reform politics one-sidedly on the immediate satisfaction of material needs in the narrowest sense. Satiated man has replaced nonalienated man as the anthropological objective of social democracy. Instead of pressing out of the realm of necessity into the realm of freedom, social democracy remains stuck in a superficial economism—thus the suspicion and the criticism. [2]

Social democracy has, in fact, achieved its most impressive results where it has been geared to a material, economic betterment of man: increasing real incomes, securing prosperity, developing the welfare state. This orientation and these successes are not to be held against social democracy; they should rather be recognized. The suspicion of hedonism charges social democracy with getting stuck in this initial sphere and with losing its perspective; if the realm of necessity is being recognizably dismantled, where then are the contours of the realm of freedom?

The notion that social democracy has become set in an all too narrow social policy and thus all too firmly embedded in existing conditions is nourished by the deficiency of its international solidarity. Social Democracy is Eurocentric. European Social Democracy has done little to break down the European ghetto. Rather, it has fallen in with Europe's role as beneficiary of the worldwide division into rich and poor.

European Social Democratic politicians, supported by Social Democratic parties, have been among those waging colonial wars. It was not the governing Social Democracy but rather Gaullism in power that granted independence for Algeria after a bloody struggle. In their policies on the Third World the governing Social Democracies of the present do not significantly distinguish themselves from their Liberal, Conservative, and Christian Democratic rivals. European Social Democracy presents itself as an out-and-out representative of privileged interests that have to be defended.

This deficiency in international solidarity by no means emanates from an insular nationalism on the part of governing Social Democracy. It is simply the consequence of the binding ties that the individual Social Democratic parties have entered into—ties to democratic rules and ties to ruling consciousness. So long as Social Democracy cannot win elections with slogans of international solidarity, it will not employ these slogans; at least it will not translate them into practice.

These ties control European Social Democracy in a way quite analogous to the situation of the major parties in the United States. When in doubt, the Democratic party and the Republican party, too, do not follow traditional principles or a specific ideology; in cases of conflict they follow the law of optimizing election chances. For this very reason there seems to be no place in the U.S. party system for an explicitly Social Democratic party. The function of the moderate left-wing party, with variations in regional accent, has already been taken up. The Democrats are already the traditional party of compensatory social policy, social equalization, and social security. Functionally, the Democratic party is thus the U.S. Social Democracy, regardless of its deficiency in socialist tradition, socialist theory, or organization corresponding to that of the European parties.

Hermann Broch, avowed sympathizer with a non-Marxist, pragmatic form of government socialism, has sketched the vision

TABLE 51: Social Democracy and International Solidarity—
Measurable Expenditure for the Third World[3]

| | Public Expenditure for the Cooperation with Developing Countries (from 1976 GNP) | | Power | |
	Percent	Position	Quotient*	Position
Austria (SPÖ)	0.10	12	2.3	4
Belgium (BSP/PSB)	0.51	6	1.3	8
Denmark (S)	0.57	5	2.9	3
Finland (SDP)	0.18	10	1.6	6
France (PS)	0.62	4	0.6	11
Germany (SPD)	0.31	8	1.2	10
Italy (PSI, PSDI)	0.16	11	0.6	11
Netherlands (PvdA)	0.82	1	1.2	9
Norway (A)	0.71	3	3.2	2
Sweden (SAP)	0.82	1	3.6	1
Switzerland (SPS)	0.19	9	1.4	7
United Kingdom (Lab)	0.38	7	1.9	5

*See Table 31.
Note: No data available for Portugal and Spain.

of a party of international "totalitarian humanitarianism." Characteristic of this utopia is that it aims to free social humanitarianism from the limits imposed upon it by national egoisms. As
long as the individual Social Democratic parties must first win
elections in their own countries, and as long as this means consideration for prejudices and privileges, then Social Democracy
will—as much as the bourgeois parties—be incapable of taking
a step toward international totalitarian humanitarianism. As
soon as Social Democracy gives up its binding ties to national
interests and its ties to democratic rules in its own country,
it gives up its power, too, losing the instruments needed for
creating humanitarianism. [4]

There is no clear, smooth road out of this contradiction.
But this vision of a party that does not remain entangled in
the thicket of national interest out of a consideration for critical
voter groups can be a guide; it can indicate the direction for
Social Democracy to gradually change the consciousness that is
hindering a breaking out from national and vulgar materialist
constraints.

Karl W. Deutsch sees a political system's capacity to learn
as dependent on the "number and diversity of unfettered aids

available to the system or the organization."[5] Social democracy has made a substantial contribution to the stability of the European political system. But in order to be able to carry out this function in the future, social democracy's ties to the existing society must not be total; social democracy must be at least to some extent unfettered—that is at least to some extent distanced.

A Social Democracy that no longer musters the strength for the vision and no longer measures the existing social order against the design of a possible future order has lost its historical mission. It has forfeited its distinctive character and its principles.

Social democracy faces the challenge of living in the future amid dialectical tensions and of bearing in future a Janus face: it must not run away from power, but neither must it give up its principles. A powerful yet unprincipled Social Democracy is a shell without substance. A principled yet impotent Social Democracy moves to the level of sects and small churches. The future of social democracy depends upon whether it is able to maintain the balance in this contradiction.

Notes

1. ON THE CONCEPT AND ORIGINS OF SOCIAL DEMOCRACY AND DEMOCRATIC SOCIALISM

1. Michael Harrington, Socialism. New York, 1972, p. 344.
2. Leszek Kolakowski, The Main Currents of Marxism: Its Rise, Growth and Dissolution. 3 vols., Munich, 1978, esp. vol. 1; Wolfgang Abendroth, A Short History of the European Working Class. New York and London, 1973, pp. 9-68; and W. Werner Ernst, Sozialdemokratie: Versuch einer Rekonstruktion. Vienna, 1979.
3. Julius Braunthal, History of the International. 3 vols., 2d ed. New York and London, 1967 and 1980, esp. vol. 1, pp. 195-254.
4. Dieter Oberndörfer, ed., Sozialistische und Kommunistische Parteien in Westeuropa. Vol. 1, Südländer. Opladen, 1978.
5. C. B. MacPherson, The Political Theory of Possessive Individualism: Hobbes to Locke. Oxford, 1962, esp. pp. 263-77; Geschichte der bürgerlichen Philosophie. Frankfurt am Main, 1973.
6. Peter Bachrach, The Theory of Democratic Elitism: A Critique. Boston, 1967, pp. 83-106; Anton Pelinka, Dynamische Demokratie: Zur konkreten Utopie gesellschaftlicher Gleichheit. Stuttgart, 1974, pp. 20-31, 58-74; and Martin Greiffenhagen, Freiheit gegen Gleichheit? Zur "Tendenzwelle" in der Bundesrepublik. Hamburg, 1975, pp. 41-60.
7. Anthony Downs, An Economic Theory of Democracy. New York, 1957.
8. Johannes Messner, "Was bedeutet 'christlich-demokratisch' heute?" in Andreas Kohl et al., ed., Um Parlament und Partei: Alfred Maleta zum 70. Geburtstag. Graz, 1976.
9. Zusammenarbeit per Parteien in Westeuropa: Auf dem Weg zu einer neuen politischen Infrastruktur? Bonn, 1976; Theo Stammen, ed., Parteien in Europa: Nationale Parteiensysteme, Transnationale Parteienbeziehungen, Konturen eines Europäischen Parteiensystems. 2nd ed., Munich, 1978; Joachim Raschke, ed., Die politischen Parteien in Westeuropa: Geschichte-Programm-Praxis. Ein Handbuch. Reinbek, 1978; Norbert Gresch, Transnationale Parteienzusammenarbeit in der EG.

Baden-Baden, 1978; and Stanley Henig, ed., Political Parties in the European Community. London, 1979.

10. Compare with the formulation in the SPÖ's New Party Program of 1978, paragraph 1.4, "Socialism is an international movement in which people work together for a better society on the basis of humanistic values, on the basis of Marxist or other methods of social analysis, or of religious convections."

11. Santiago Carrillo, Eurocommunism and the State. Westport, Conn., 1978, esp. pp. 77-109.

Heinz Timmermann, ed., Eurokommunismus. Fakten, Analysen, Interviews. Frankfurt am Main, 1978.

2. HISTORY OF IDEAS IN SOCIAL DEMOCRACY

1. C. Wright Mills, The Marxists, New York, 1963, p. 473.

2. Leszek Kolakowski, The Main Currents of Marxism: Its Rise, Growth and Dissolution, vol. 1. Munich, 1978, esp. pp. 100-07.

3. Adam Schaff, Marxismus und das menschliche Individuum. Vienna, 1965; Arnold Künzli, Karl Marx: Eine Psychographie. Vienna, 1966; and Fritz J. Raddatz, Karl Marx: A Political Biography. Boston, 1979.

4. Wolfgang Abendroth, A Short History of the European Working Class. New York and London, 1973, pp. 27-50; Norbert Leser, Die Odyssee des Marxismus: Auf dem Weg zum Sozialismus. Vienna, 1971, esp. pp. 13-48; Gesine Schwan, Die Gesellschaftskritik von Karl Marx: Politökonomische und philosophische voraussetzungen. Stuttgart, 1974; and Michael Harrington, Socialism. New York, 1972, esp. pp. 36-108.

5. Compare with, in general, George Macauley Trevelyan, British History in the Nineteenth Century and After (1782-1919). Harmondsworth, 1971.

6. Norbert Leser, Begegnung und Auftrag: Beiträge zur Orientierung im zeitgenössischen Sozialismus. Vienna, 1963, pp. 173-85.

7. Johannes Messner, Das Englische Experiment des Sozialismus: Auf Grund ökonomischer Tatsachen und sozialistischer Selbstzeugnisse dargestellt. Innsbruck, 1954, esp. pp. 11-18; Lewis Minkin and Patrick Seyd, "The British Labour Party" in William E. Paterson and Alastair H. Thomas, eds., Social Democratic Parties in Western Europe. London, 1977; David Howell, British Social Democracy: A Study in Development and Decay. London, 1976, esp. pp. 9-46; and Ralph Miliband,

Parliamentary Socialism: A Study in the Politics of Labour. 2d ed., London, 1973.

8. Eduard Bernstein, Sozialdemokratische Lehrjahre: Nachdruck. West Berlin, 1978; Kolakowski, Main Currents, vol. 2, pp. 98-353; and Sven Papcke, Der Revisionismusstreit und die politische Theorie der Reform: Fragen und Vergleiche. Stuttgart, 1979.

9. Kolakowski, Main Currents, vol. 1, pp. 182-244.

10. Julius Braunthal, History of the International. Vol. 2, New York and London, 1967; and Abendroth, European Working Class, pp. 69-100.

11. Compare with Lenin's polemic against the "compromises of Social Democracy with the bandits." Vladimir I. Lenin, "Left-Wing Communism, An Infantile Disorder" in Collected Works. Vol. 31, Moscow, London, 1966, p. 37.

12. Otto Bauer, "Zwischen zwei Weltkriegen?" in Werkausgabe, vol. 4. Vienna, 1976, esp. pp. 296-315. At this juncture (1936) Bauer is attempting to construct a theoretical bridge to communism.

13. Maurice Duverger, Political Parties: Their Organization and Activity in the Modern State, 2d ed., New York, 1959, p. 235. He speaks of "sinistrisme" (leftism) in this context.

14. Susanne Miller, Die SPD vor und nach Godesberg. Bonn, 1974; and Wolfgang Abendroth, Aufstieg und Krise der deutschen sozialdemokratie. Das problem der zweckentfremdung einer politischen Partei durch die Anpassungstendenz von institutionen an vorgegebene Machtverhältnisse. Cologne, 1978, esp. pp. 69-92.

15. This classification essentially follows the two-part division in Dieter Oberndörfer, Hans Rühle, and Hans-Joachim Veen, eds., Sozialistische und Kommunistische Parteien in Westeuropa. 2 vols. Opladen, 1978, 1979. Socialism in the countries of the South (vol. 1) largely coincides with predominance of opposition socialism.

16. In part from Wolfgang Leonhard, Die dreispaltung des Marxismus: Ursprung und Entwicklung des Sowjetmarxismus, Maoismus und Reformkommunismus. Düsseldorf, 1970. See the illustration on the inside front cover.

3. DEVELOPMENT OF SOCIAL DEMOCRATIC AND SOCIALIST PARTIES

1. Maurice Duverger, Political Parties: Their Organization and Activity in the Modern State, New York, 1959, p. 235.

2. The "Siamese twins" characterization of the relation-ship between a Social Democratic party and free trade unions goes back to Victor Adler. Cited in Kurt L. Shell, The Trans-formation of Austrian Socialism. New York, 1962, p. 59.

3. On party typology in general, compare Duverger, Political Parties; Maurice Duverger, Party Politics and Pressure Groups: A Comparative Introduction. London, 1972; and Kurt Lenk and Franz Neumann, eds., Theorie und Soziologie der politischen Parteien. Neuwied, 1968.

4. Leszek Kolakowski, The Main Currents of Marxism: Its Rise, Growth and Dissolution, vol. 2. Oxford, 1978, pp. 384-98.

5. Norbert Leser, Die Odyssee des Marxismus: Auf dem Weg zum Sozialismus. Vienna, 1971, pp. 49-229.

6. On the U.S. development in this regard, see C. Wright Mills, White Collar: The American Middle Classes. London, New York, 1951.

7. These essential tensions are described also in Günther Nenning, Realisten oder Verräter? Die Zukunft der Sozialdemo-kratie. Munich, 1976.

8. Joachim Raschke, Organisierter Konflikt in West-europäischen Parteien: Vergleichende Analyse Parteiinterner Oppositionsgruppen. Opladen, 1977, p. 266; and William E. Paterson and Alastair H. Thomas, eds., Social Democratic Parties in Western Europe. London, 1977.

9. Otto Kirchheimer, "Der Weg zur Allerweltspartei," in Lenk and Neumann, Theorie, pp. 345-367.

10. Giovanni Sartori, "The Case of Polarized Pluralism," in Joseph La Palombara and Myron Econ Weiner, eds., Political Parties and Political Development. Princeton, 1966.

11. Jean Blondel, An Introduction to Comparative Govern-ment. London, 1969, pp. 155-60.

12. On the left Socialist type of party, compare with Raschke, Organisierter Konflikt, pp. 76-79.

13. Data based on Joachim Raschke, ed., Die politischen Parteien in Westeuropa: Geschichte, Programm, Praxis. Ein Handbuch. Reinbek, 1978, and supplemented by subsequent results of parliamentary elections in France, Finland, the United Kingdom, Austria, Sweden, Switzerland, Denmark, and Portugal. This election data is in part from Economist, the Neue Züricher Zeitung, and the Portuguese embassy in Vienna. Compare also Theo Stammen, ed., Parteien in Europa: Nationale Parteien-systeme, Transnationale Parteienbeziehungen, Konturen eines Europäischen Parteiensystems, 2d ed. Munich, 1978; as well as Paterson and Thomas, Social Democratic Parties.

4. ELECTORATE AND MEMBERSHIP

1. Robert Michels, "Formale Demokratie und oligarchische Wirklichkeit," in Kurt Lenk and Franz Neumann, eds., Theorie und Soziologie der politischen Parteien. Neuwied, 1968, p. 257.

2. Compiled from Socialist Affairs, Socialist International Information, 2/1979, p. 56. The compilation reflects the situation as of the spring of 1979.

3. Compare in general William E. Paterson and Alastair H. Thomas, eds., Social Democratic Parties in Western Europe. London, 1977; Joachim Raschke, ed., Die politischen Parteien in Westeuropa: Geschichte, Programm, Praxis. Ein Handbuch. Reinbek, 1978; Theo Stammen, ed., Parteien in Europa: Nationale Parteiensysteme, Transnationale Parteienbeziehungen, Konturen eines Europäischen Parteiensystems, 2d ed. Munich, 1978.

4. Maurice Duverger, Political Parties: Their Organization and Activity in the Modern State. New York, 1959, pp. 5-17.

5. Data based on Raschke, Die politischen Parteien.

6. Jürgen Hartmann, "Grossbritanien," in Raschke, Die politischen Parteien, pp. 258-60; compare also David Howell, British Social Democracy: A Study in Development and Decay. London, 1976.

7. Karl Kuhn, "Norwegen," and Christian Fenner, "Schweden," in Raschke, Die politischen Parteien, pp. 397-411, pp. 452-477.

8. Duverger, Political Parties, pp. 23-40.

9. Projektgruppe Parteiensystem (Zentralinstitut für sozialwissenschaftliche Forschung der FU Berlin), "Bundesrepublik Deutschland," in Raschke, Die politischen Parteien, p. 106.

10. Data based on Raschke, Die politischen Parteien, supplemented by the results of subsequent parliamentary elections in France, Finland, Spain (1979), the United Kingdom, Austria, and Sweden (1979).

11. Reto Pieth, "Schweiz," in Raschke, Die politischen Parteien, pp. 478-95.

12. See note 10.

13. According to the data in Table 7 and in Duverger, Political Parties, p. 95.

14. Compare Albrecht Langner, ed., Katholizismus und freiheitlicher Sozialismus in Europa. Cologne, 1965; and Marcel Reding, Der politische Atheismus, 2d ed. Graz, 1958.

15. Richard Rose, ed., Electoral Behavior: A Comparative Handbook. New York, 1974, pp. 92-94, 156, 190, 255, 276, 306-08, 364, 428, 507, and 521.

16. Joachim Raschke, Organisierter Konflikt in West-
europäischen Parteien: Vergleichende Analyse Parteiinterner
Oppositionsgruppen. Opladen, 1977, p. 266.

17. Joachim Raschke, Die politischen Parteien; and Byron
Criddle, "The French Parti Socialiste," in William E. Paterson
and Alastair H. Thomas, eds., Social Democratic Parties in
Western Europe. London, 1977, p. 59.

18. Raschke, Die politischen Parteien, pp. 76, 126.

19. Raschke, Organisierter Konflikt, p. 266.

20. Projektgruppe Parteiensystem, "Bundesrepublik
Deutschland," p. 103.

21. Samuel H. Barnes, Italy: Religion and Class in Electoral Behavior," in Rose, Electoral Behavior, p. 190.

22. Anton Pelinka, "Österreich," in Raschke, Die politischen
Parteien, p. 417.

23. Richard Rose, "Britain: Simple Abstractions and Com-
plex Realities," in Rose, Electoral Behavior, p. 518; and Arend
Lijphart, "The Netherlands: Continuity and Change in Voting
Behavior," in Rose, Electoral Behavior, p. 246.

24. Bo Särlvik, "Sweden: The Social Bases of the Parties
in a Developmental Perspective," in Rose, Electoral Behavior,
p. 418.

25. Compare in general Lynne B. Iglitzin and Ruth Ross,
eds., Women in the World: A Comparative Study. Santa Barbara,
Calif., 1976.

26. Criddle, "French Parti Socialiste," p. 59; Barnes,
"Italy," p. 192; Lijphart, "Netherlands," p. 255; and Särlvik,
"Sweden," p. 428.

27. Economist, May 12, 1979, p. 26; and IMAS-Report,
October 6, 1975, p. 3.

28. Nils Diederich, "Zur Mitgliederstruktur von CDU und
SPD," in Jürgen Dittberner and Rolf Ebbighausen, Parteiensystem in der Legitimationskrise: Studien und Materialien zur
Soziologie der Parteien in der Bundesrepublik Deutschland.
Opladen, 1973, esp. p. 42. Compare also the even slightly
declining proportion of women within the SPÖ membership over
a longer period, from 35.5 percent on December 31, 1945, to
33.8 percent on December 31, 1977. Jahrbuch 1978, Bericht
an den 24. ordentlichen Bundesparteitag der SPÖ, Statistiken.

29. Särlvik, "Sweden," p. 404.

30. Mattei Dogan, "Political Cleavage and Social Stratification in France and Italy," in Seymour M. Lipset and Stein Rokkan,
eds., Party Systems and Voter Alignments: Cross-national Perspectives. New York, 1967, esp. pp. 131-41.

31. Robert R. McKenzie and Allan Silver, "The Delicate Experiment: Industrialism, Conservatism and Working-Class Tories in England," in Lipset and Rokkan, Party Systems, p. 124.

32. Duverger, Political Parties, pp. 71-79.

33. Jürgen Hartmann, "Grossbritanien," p. 260.

34. Anton Pelinka, "Österreich," p. 419.

35. Werner Herzog, "Portugal," in Raschke, Die politischen Parteien, p. 440.

36. Uwe Schleth, Parteifinanzen: Eine Studie über Kosten und finanzierung der Parteitätigkeit, zu deren politischer Problematik und zu den möglichkeiten einer Reform. Meisenheim, 1973, p. 255.

37. Klaus von Beyme, Das politische System der Bundesrepublik Deutschland: Eine Einführung. Munich, 1979, p. 81.

38. G. D. H. Cole, A History of the Labour Party from 1914. London, 1978, pp. 151 and 249.

39. John Sanford, The Mass Media of the German-Speaking Countries. London, 1976, pp. 9 and 49.

40. Norbert Lepszy, Regierung, Parteien und Gewerkschaften in den Niederlanden: Entwicklung und Strukturen. Düsseldorf, 1979, pp. 41 and 311.

41. Rudolf Steininger, Polarisierung und Integration: Eine vergleichende Untersuchung der strukturellen Versäulung der Gesellschaft in den Niederlanden und in Österreich. Meisenheim, 1975.

42. Robert Michels, Zur Soziologie des Parteiwesens in der modernen Demokratie, 2d ed. Leipzig, 1925.

43. Jürgen Hartmann, "Grossbritanien," p. 258.

44. Projektgruppe Parteiensystem, "Bundesrepublik Deutschland," p. 106.

45. Klaus Hänsch, "Frankreich," in Raschke, Die politischen Parteien, p. 182.

46. Joachim Raschke, Organisierter Konflikt, p. 266; compare also Criddle, "The French Parti Socialiste," p. 62.

47. Colin Mellors, The British MP: A Socio-economic Study of the House of Commons. Westmead, 1978, pp. 50, 62-66; compare also in general Tom Forester, The British Labour Party and the Working Class. New York, 1976.

48. Mellors, British MP, p. 107; Lieselotte Berger, Lenelotte von Bothmer, and Helga Schuchardt, Frauen ins Parlament? Von den schwierigkeiten, gleichberechtigt zu sein. Reinbek, 1976, p. 85.

49. Fenner, "Schweden," p. 460; and Knut Heidar, "The Norwegian Labour Party: Social Democracy in a Periphery of

Europe," in Paterson and Thomas, Social Democratic Parties, p. 313.

50. Duverger, Political Parties, pp. 156-57.

51. Jahrbuch 1978, Bericht an den 24. ordentlichen Bundesparteitag der SPÖ, Statistiken; Melanie A. Sully, "The Socialist Party of Austria," in Paterson and Thomas, Social Democratic Parties, p. 219.

52. Raschke, Organisierter Konflikt, pp. 86 and 177.

53. Jürgen Hartmann, "Belgien," in Raschke, Die politischen Parteien, pp. 54-59; Xavier Mabille and Val R. Lorwin, "The Belgian Socialist Party," in Paterson and Thomas, Social Democratic Parties, pp. 389-407.

54. Hartmann, "Grossbritanien," pp. 261-66; Lewis Minkin and Patrick Seyd, "The British Labour Party," in Paterson and Thomas, Social Democratic Parties, pp. 117-22.

55. Detlef Murphy and Heinz Timmermann, "Italien," in Raschke, Die politischen Parteien, pp. 351-53; David Hine, "Social Democracy in Italy," in Paterson and Thomas, Social Democratic Parties, pp. 74-77.

56. Projektgruppe Parteiensystem, "Bundesrepublik Deutschland," p. 109; Karl Kuhn, "Norwegen," p. 404.

57. Raschke, Organisierter Konflikt, p. 197.

58. Karl-Heinz Naßmacher, "Linke Volkspartei und Klassengesellschaft," in Norbert Gansel, ed., Überwindet den Kapitalismus oder Was wollen die Jungsozialisten? Reinbek, 1971; also, in general, Hans Mommsen, ed., Sozialdemokratie zwischen Klassenbewegung und Volkspartei. Frankfurt am Main, 1974; compare also in this regard, as an example of internal party communication, the study SPD-Mitglieder 1977. Eine Bestandsaufnahme von Aktivitäten, Einstellungen und Kommunikationsverhalten. INFAS Report. Bonn, 1977.

5. GOVERNMENT AND OPPOSITION ROLES

1. Eduard Bernstein, "Evolutionärer Sozialismus," in Helmut Hirsch, Der "Fabier" Eduard Bernstein: Zur Entwicklungsgeschichte des evolutionären Sozialismus. West Berlin, 1977, p. 127.

2. On the definition of concepts, compare Klaus von Beyme, Die parlamentarischen Regierungssysteme in Europa. Munich, 1970, pp. 29-48.

3. Karl-Heinz Naßmacher, Politikwissenschaft I: Politische Systeme und politische Soziologie, 2d ed. Düsseldorf, 1973, pp. 33-37.

4. Constructed on the basis of the data in Beyme, Die parlamentarischen, pp. 901-67; and in Joachim Raschke, ed., Die politischen Parteien in Westeuropa: Geschichte, Program, Praxis. Ein Handbuch. Reinbek, 1978.

5. Compare with Chapter 4.

6. Projektgruppe Parteiensystem (Zentralinstitut für sozialwissenschaftliche Forschung der FU Berlin), "Bundesrepublik Deutschland," in Raschke, Die politischen Parteien, p. 105; Lewis Minkin and Patrick Seyd, "The British Labour Party," in William E. Paterson and Alastair H. Thomas, ed., Social Democratic Parties in Western Europe. London, 1977, p. 149.

7. Allen Hutt, British Trade Unionism: A Short History. London, 1975.

8. Thomas Lachs, Wirtschaftspartnerschaft in Österreich. Vienna, 1976.

9. Susanne Miller, Die SPD vor und nach Godesberg. Bonn, 1974.

10. Kurt L. Shell, The Transformation of Austrian Socialism. New York, 1962; Felix Kreissler, "Die Entwicklung der SPÖ in ihren Programmen und in ihrer Politik: Vom Austromarxismus zum 'Austrosozialismus' (1945-1973). Wähler, Mitglieder, Funktionäre und Mandatare," in Gerhard Botz, Hans Hautmann, and Helmut Konrad, eds., Geschichte und Gesellschaft: Festschrift fur Karl R. Stadler zum 60. Geburtstag. Vienna, 1974.

11. Karl W. Deutsch, Politics and Government: How People Decide Their Fate. Boston, 1970, pp. 334-60.

12. Compiled from Wirtschafts- und sozialstatistisches Taschenbuch 1979, Österreichischer Arbeiterkammertag. Vienna, 1979, p. 46.

13. Wirtschafts- und sozialstatistisches Taschenbuch 1979, p. 56.

14. Wirtschafts- und sozialstatistisches Taschenbuch 1979, p. 26.

15. Wirtschafts- und sozialstatistisches Taschenbuch 1979, p. 25.

16. Wirtschafts- und sozialstatistisches Taschenbuch 1979, pp. 24 and 38.

17. OECD tabulation of December 30, 1977; Education Committee, Education Policies and Trends in the Context of Social and Economic Development Perspectives. Analytical Report. For Austria: Report of the Federal Ministry for Science and Research, Division of Planning and Statistics.

18. Manfred G. Schmidt, Die Regulierung des Kapitalismus unter burgerlichen und sozialdemokratischen Regierungen. Ein Beitrag zur Analyse des Steuerstaates, des Wohlfahrtstaates und der Lage auf dem Arbeitsmarkt. Diskussionsbeitrag Nr. 8/79, Univ. Constance, Department of Political Science and Public Administration.

19. von Beyme, Die parlamentarischen, pp. 901-67; Raschke, Die politischen Parteien.

20. Ibid.

21. Compiled from von Beyme, Die parlamentarischen, pp. 901-67; and Raschke, Die politischen Parteien.

22. Detlef Murphy and Heinz Timmermann, "Italien," in Raschke, Die politischen Parteien, pp. 345-57.

23. The data are based on figures calculated for roughly the mid-1970s in Joachim Raschke, Organisierter Konflikt in Westeuropäischen Parteien: Vergleichende Analyse Parteiinterner Oppositionsgruppen. Opladen, 1977. For the Netherlands and Switzerland, supplementary calculations from election results in Raschke, Die politischen Parteien, pp. 396 and 495.

24. Cited in Shell, Transformation, p. 59.

25. This split is still reflected today in the antagonisms between the Communist-oriented World Federation of Trade Unions (WFTU) and the Social Democratic-oriented International Confederation of Free Trade Unions (ICFTU). On this, Alfred Ströer, Solidarität international: Der ÖGB und die internationale Gewerkschaftsbewegung. Vienna, 1977.

26. The Christian Democratic alignment unions are organized in the World Confederation of Labour (WCL), the successor organization to the International Federation of Christian Trade Unions (IFCTU). Ströer, Solidarität international.

27. Joachim Raschke, Organisierter Konflikt, esp. p. 278.

28. Klaus von Beyme, Interessengruppen in der Demokratie. Munich, 1969; and idem, Gewerkschaften und Arbeitsbeziehungen in kapitalistischen Landern. Munich, 1977.

29. von Beyme, Gewerkschaften, pp. 44-60.

30. von Beyme, Gewerkschaften, p. 78; on the relations of the individual parties to the unions, compare William E. Paterson and Alastair H. Thomas, eds., Social Democratic Parties in Western Europe. London, 1977.

31. Klaus Hänsch, "Frankreich," in Raschke, Die politischen Parteien, p. 181; and Detlef Murphy and Heinz Timmermann, "Italien," in Raschke, Die politischen Parteien, pp. 349 and 356.

32. von Beyme, Gewerkschaften, p. 78; and Wirtschafts- und sozialstatistisches Taschenbuch 1979, Österreichischer Arbeiterkammertag. Vienna, 1979, p. 44.

33. Allen Hutt, British Trade Unionism.

34. Raschke, Organisierter Konflikt, pp. 85-88.

35. Anton Pelinka, Gewerkschaften im Parteienstaat: Ein Vergleich zwischen dem Deutschen und dem Österreichischen Gewerkschaftsbund. West Berlin, 1980.

36. Hans J. Kleinsteuber, Die USA—Politik, Wirtschaft, Gesellschaft: Eine Einführung. Hamburg, 1974, pp. 46-50.

37. Jürgen Hartmann, "Grossbritanien," in Raschke, Die politischen Parteien, p. 259.

38. Gerhard Lehmbruch, Proporzdemokratie: Politisches System und politische Kultur in der Schweiz und in Österreich. Tübingen, 1967; Arend Lijphart, The Politics of Accommodation: Pluralism and Democracy in the Netherlands. Berkeley, 1968; Rudolf Steininger, Polarisierung und Integration: Eine vergleichende Untersuchung der strukturellen Versäulung der Gesellschaft in den Niederlanden und in Österreich. Meisenheim, 1975.

39. Jahrbuch 1978, Bericht an den 24. ordenlichen Bundesparteitag der SPÖ. Vienna, 1978.

40. Christian Fenner, "Schweden," in Raschke, Die politischen Parteien, p. 461

41. Hermann Adam, Die Konzertierte Aktion in der Bundesrepublik. Cologne, 1972.

42. Julius Braunthal, History of the International, vol. 1, New York and London, 1967, pp. 95-194.

43. Braunthal, History, vol. 1, pp. 195-242.

44. Braunthal, History, vol. 2, pp. 149-270.

45. Braunthal, History, vol. 2, p. 333.

46. Braunthal, History, vol. 3, pp. 182-212.

47. Braunthal, History, vol. 2, pp. 468-92.

48. Socialist Affairs, 2/1979, p. 56

49. Socialist Affairs, 2/1979, p. 2.

50. Braunthal, History, vol. 3, p. 197. The Labour party of Malta is considered a European party.

51. Hans Janitschek, "Zur Entwicklung und Tätigkeit der Sozialistischen Internationale," in Andreas Khol and Alfred Stirnemann, eds., Österreichisches Jahrbuch für Politik 1978. Vienna, 1979, p. 206.

52. Theo Stammen, ed., Parteien in Europa. Nationale Parteiensysteme, Transnationale Parteienbeziehungen, Konturen eines Europäischen Parteiensystems, 2d ed. Munich, 1978, p. 277; and Janitschek, "Zur Entwicklung," p. 113.

53. Compiled from Economist, June 16, 1979, pp. 25-33.

54. Braunthal, History, vol. 3, pp. 366-74.

55. Compare the individual studies in Werner J. Feld, ed., The Foreign Policies of West European Socialist Parties. New York, 1978; in Paterson and Thomas, Social Democratic Parties; and in Raschke, Die politischen Parteien.

56. Cited in Khol and Stirnemann, Österreichisches Jahrbuch, p. 234.

57. Volker Bornschier, Wachstum, Konzentration und Multinationalisierung von Industrieunternehmen. Frauenfeld, 1976, p. 562.

58. Braunthal, History, vol. 3, pp. 45-67 and 189-91.

59. Jonathan Story, "Social Revolution and Democracy in Iberia," in Paterson and Thomas, Social Democratic Parties, pp. 86-100; and Thomas C. Bruneau, "The Portuguese Socialists: Restructuring Portuguese Foreign Policy," in Feld, Foreign Policies, pp. 102-21.

60. Compiled from the data in Feld, Foreign Policies; Paterson and Thomas, Social Democratic Parties; and Raschke, Die politischen Parteien.

61. Feld, Foreign Policies, p. 148.

62. Bruno Kreisky, Die Zeit, in der wir leben: Betrachtungen zur internationalen Politik. Vienna, 1978.

6. PROGRAMMATIC TRADITIONS

1. Bertrand Russell, German Social Democracy. New York, 1965, p. 170.

2. Ossip K. Flechtheim, "Parteiprogramme," in Kurt Lenk and Franz Neumann, Theorie und Soziologie der politischen Parteien. Neuwied, 1968.

3. Heinrich Potthof, Die Sozialdemokratie von den Anfängen bis 1945. Bonn, 1974, pp. 25-60.

4. G. D. H. Cole, British Working-class Politics, 1832-1914. London, 1941; and idem, A History of the Labour Party from 1914. London, 1978.

5. Julius Braunthal, History of the International, vol. 3. London, 1980, p. 533.

6. Ralph Miliband, Parliamentary Socialism: A Study in the Politics of Labour, 2d ed. London, 1973, esp. pp. 272-317; and Tom Forester, The British Labour Party and the Working Class. New York, 1976, pp. 52-67.

7. Byron Criddle, "The French Parti Socialiste," in William E. Paterson and Alastair H. Thomas, eds., Social Democratic Parties in Western Europe. London, 1977, p. 26.

8. Udo Bermbach, "Rätegedanken versus Parlamentaris-
mus? Überlegungen zur aktuellen Diskussion der Neuen Linken;"
and Peter von Oertzen, "Freiheitliche demokratische Grundord-
nung und Rätesystem," in Udo Bermbach, ed., Theorie und
Praxis der direkten Demokratie: Texte und Materialien zur
Räte-Diskussion. Opladen, 1973.

9. Wolfgang Jäger, "Die Sozialistische und die Kommunistische Partei Frankreichs," in Dieter Oberndörfer, Hans
Ruhle, and Hans Joachim Veen, eds., Sozialistische und Kommunistische Parteien in Westeuropa, Vol. 1. Opladen, 1978,
esp. pp. 93-100.

10. Braunthal, History, vol. 3, p. 534.

11. Braunthal, History, vol. 3, pp. 187-89.

12. Braunthal, History, vol. 3, pp. 45-67 and 189-91.

13. Braunthal, History, vol. 3, p. 534.

14. Compare Charles Levinson, ed., Industry's Democratic
Revolution. London, 1974; and Fritz Vilmar, ed., Industrielle
Demokratie in Westeuropa: Menschenwürde im Betrieb II.
Reinbek, 1975.

15. Albrecht Langner, ed., Katholizismus und freiheitlicher Sozialismus in Europa. Cologne, 1965; and Franz Klüber,
Katholische Soziallehre und demokratischer Sozialismus. Bonn,
1974.

16. Braunthal, History, vol. 3, p. 533.

17. Jäger, "Die Sozialistische"; Criddle, "The French
Parti Socialiste;" and Klaus Hänsch, "Frankreich," in Joachim
Raschke, ed., Die politischen Parteien in Westeuropa: Geschichte,
Programm, Praxis. Ein Handbuch. Reinbek, 1978.

18. Compare the illustration for the period of 1950 in
Maurice Duverger, Political Parties: Their Organization and
Activity in the Modern State. New York, 1959, p. 232.

19. Susanne Miller, Die SPD vor und nach Godesberg.
Bonn, 1974. For example, the Greek PASOK has rejected
membership in the Socialist International primarily because it
regards the SPD as a "representative of monopoly capitalism
and the US." See also Ilias Katsoulis, "Griechenland," in
Raschke, Die politischen Parteien, p. 232.

20. Friedrich A. Hayek, The Road to Serfdom. Chicago,
1944.

21. Compare the arguments of Wilhelm Hennis, Demokrati-
sierung: Zur Problematik eines Begriffs. Cologne, 1970.
Central to this position is an emphatic distinction between state
and society. See also Wilhelm Hennis, Organisierter Sozialismus:
Zum "strategischen" Staats- und Politikverständnis der sozialdemokratie. Stuttgart, 1977.

On the British critique from the right, see Neill Nugent and Roger King, eds., The British Right: Conservative and Right Wing Politics in Britain. Westmead, 1977, pp. 29-129.

22. Jean-Francois Revel, The Totalitarian Temptation. New York, 1977; compare also in general Oberndörfer, Sozialstiche.

23. Revel, Totalitarian Temptation, p. 214.

24. Alexander Schwan and Gesine Schwan, Sozialdemokratie und Marxismus: Zum Spannungsverhältnis von Godesberger Programm und Marxistischer Theorie. Hamburg, 1974, p. 171.

25. Rudolf Wohlgenannt, Der demokratische Sozialismus: Sein Selbstverständnis und sein Verhältnis zum Marxismus. Vienna, 1978, p. 114.

26. Arnold Künzli, Tradition und Revolution: Zur Theorie eines nichmarxistischen Sozialismus. Basel, 1975; similarly see Norbert Leser, Die Odyssee des Marxismus: Auf dem Weg zum Sozialismus. Vienna, 1971.

27. Vladimir Granov, "Die Krise der Ideologie des Sozialreformismus," in Die gegenwartige Sozialdemokratie: Neue sowjetische Analysen. Cologne, 1973, p. 101; Alfred Bönisch and Dieter Reichelt, Burgerliche Gesellschaftskonzeptionen und Wirklichkeit. Berlin, 1976, pp. 148-69.

28. Santiago Carrillo, "Eurocommunism" and the State. Westport, Conn., 1978, pp. 103-04.

29. Johannes Agnoli and Peter Brückner, Die Transformation der Demokratie. Frankfurt am Main, 1974, p. 77.

30. Miliband, Parliamentary Socialism, p. 372.

31. Peter von Oertzen, "Thesen zur Strategie und Taktik des Demokratischen Sozialismus in der Bundesrepublik Deutschland," in Georg Lührs, ed., Beiträge zur Theoriediskussion II. West Berlin, 1974, p. 48.

32. Egon Matzner, Wohlfahrtsstaat und Wirtschaftskrise: Österreichs Sozialisten suchen einen Ausweg. Reinbek, 1978, p. 104. Compare also the left position, based on economic analyses, in Eduard März, Einführung in die Marxsche Theorie der Wirtschaftlichen Entwicklung. Vienna, 1976.

33. As representative of positions of the Social Democratic middle in the German discussion, compare Heiner Flohr, Klaus Lompe, and Lothar F. Neumann, Freiheitlicher Sozialismus: Beiträge zu seinem heutigen Selbstverständnis. Bonn, 1973; for the Austrian discussion, see Heinz Fischer, Positionen und Perspektiven. Vienna, 1977.

34. Cited in Walter Menningen, ed., Ungleichheit im Wohlfahrtsstaat: Der Alva-Myrdal-Report der Schwedischen Sozialdemokraten. Reinbek, 1971, p. 48.

35. On the function of ideology in the multiparty system, compare in general Anthony Downs, An Economic Theory of Democracy. New York, 1957.

36. Cited in Jean-Claude Criqui, "Der franzosische Sozialismus," in Langner, Katholizismus, p. 124.

37. Jäger, "Die Sozialistische," pp. 55-61; Criddle, "The French Parti Socialiste."

38. Albert Kadan and Anton Pelinka, Die Grundsatzpro- gramm der Österreichischen Parteien. St. Pölten, 1979, p. 144; see also Norbert Leser, Gottes Spuren in Österreich: Mein Verhältnis zum (politischen) Katholizismus. Vienna, 1978.

39. This interest of the church is analyzed in August M. Knoll, Katholische Kirche und scholastisches Naturrecht: Zur Frage der Freiheit. Vienna, 1962.

40. Hans Janitschek, "Zur Entwicklung und Tätigkeit der Sozialistischen Internationale," in Andreas Khol and Alfred Stirnemann, eds., Österreichisches Jahrbuch fur Politik 1978. Vienna, 1979, p. 200.

41. Susanne Miller, SPD, p. 118.

42. Jäger, "Die Sozialistische," pp. 65-68.

43. David W. Abbott and Edward T. Rogowsky, eds., Political Parties: Leadership, Organization, Linkage. Chicago, 1971; and Thomas A. Reilly and Michael W. Sigall, eds., New Patterns in American Politics. New York, 1975.

7. THE FUTURE OF SOCIAL DEMOCRACY

1. Hermann Broch, "Der Intellektuelle im Ost-West Kon- flikt," in Broch, Politische Schriften: Kommentierte Ausgabe. Frankfurt am Main, 1978, p. 488.

2. Harry Hoefnagels, "Der Katholik und der demokratische Sozialismus," in Herwig Büchele, Harry Hoefnagels, and Bruno Kreisky, Kirche und demokratischer Sozialismus. Vienna, 1978.

3. Bundesministerium fur wirtschaftliche Zusammenarbeit, Dritter Bericht zur Entwicklung der Bundesregierung, Deutscher Bundestag—8. Wahlperiode. Printed paper 8/1185, p. 147.

4. Hermann Broch, "Die Demokratie im Zeitalter der Versklavung," in Broch, Politische Schriften, pp. 188-90; compare also the somewhat analogous arguments in Ossip K. Flechtheim, "Haben die Parteien noch eine Zukunft?" in Aus Politik und Zeitgeschichte, supplement to the weekly Das Parla- ment, January 5, 1974.

5. Karl W. Deutsch, Politische Kybernetik: Modelle und Perspektiven, 2d ed. Freiburg, 1970, p. 152.

Bibliography

Abbott, David W., and Edward T. Rogowsky, eds. Political
   Parties: Leadership, Organization, Linkage. Chicago:
   McNally, 1971.

Abendroth, Wolfgang. Austieg und Krise der deutschen sozialdemokratie: Das problem der zweckentfremdung einer
   politischen Partei durch die anpassungstendenz von institutionen an vorgegebene Machtverhältnisse. Cologne:
   Pahl-Rugenstein, 1978.

_____. Sozialgeschichte der europäischen Arbeiterbewegung.
   Frankfurt am Main: Suhrkamp, 1965.

Bachrach, Peter. The Theory of Democratic Elitism: A Critique.
   Boston: Little, Brown, 1967.

Bauer, Otto. "Zwischen zwei Weltkriegen?" In Werkausgabe,
   Volume 4. Vienna: Europa, 1976.

Berger, Lieselotte, Lenelotte von Bothmer, and Helga Schuchardt.
   Frauen ins Parlament? Von den schwierigkeiten, gleichberechtigt zu sein. Reinbek: Rowohlt, 1976.

Bernstein, Eduard. Sozialdemokratische Lehrjahre: Nachdruck.
   West Berlin: Dietz, 1978.

Blondel, Jean. Political Parties: A Genuine Case for Discontent?
   London: Wildwood House, 1978.

_____. An Introduction to Comparative Government. London:
   Weidenfeld and Nicolson, 1969.

Bornschier, Volker. Wachstrum, Konzentration und Multinationalisierung von Industrieunternehmen. Frauenfeld:
   Huber, 1976.

Braunthal, Julius. Geschichte der Internationale, 3 vols., 2d
   ed. West Berlin: Dietz, 1974.

Brown, B. E., ed. Eurocommunism and Eurosocialism: The Left Confronts Modernity. New York: Cyrco Press, 1979.

Carrillo, Santiago. "Eurokommunismus" und Staat. Hamburg: VSA, 1977.

Castles, Francis G. The Social Democratic Image of Society: A Study of the Achievements and Origins of Scandinavian Social Democracy in Comparative Perspective. London: Routledge and Kegan Paul, 1978.

Cole, G. D. H. A History of the Labour Party from 1914. London: Routledge and Kegan Paul, 1978.

Deutsch, Karl W. Politics and Government: How People Decide Their Fate. Boston: Houghton Mifflin, 1970.

Dorfman, Gerald A. Government Versus Trade Unionism in British Politics Since 1968. Stanford: Hoover Institute Press, 1979.

Downs, Anthony. An Economic Theory of Democracy. New York: Harper & Row, 1957.

Duverger, Maurice. Political Parties, Their Organization and Activity in the Modern State. Cambridge: Methuen, 1967.

Ernst, W. Werner. Sozialdemokratie: Versuch einer Rekonstruktion. Vienna: Böhlau, 1979.

Feld, Werner J., ed. The Foreign Policies of West European Socialist Parties. New York: Praeger, 1978.

Fischer, Heinz. Positionen und Perspektiven. Vienna: Europa, 1977.

Forester, Tom. The British Labour Party and the Working Class. New York: Holmes & Meier, 1976.

Godson, Roy, and Stephen Haseler. "Eurocommunism": Implications for East and West. London: Macmillan, 1978.

Gresch, Norbert. Transnationale Parteienzusammenarbeit in der EG. Baden-Baden: Nomos, 1978.

Harrington, Michael. Socialism. New York: Saturday Review Press, 1973.

Henig, Stanley, ed. Political Parties in the European Community. London: George Allen and Unwin, 1979.

Hennis, Wilhelm. Organisierter Sozialismus: Zum "strategischen" Staats- und Politikverständnis der sozialdemokratie. Stuttgart: Klett, 1977.

Hewitt, Christopher. "The Effect of Political Democracy and Social Democracy on Equality in Industrial Societies: A Cross-national Comparison." American Sociological Review 42 (1977): 450-64.

Howell, David. British Social Democracy: A Study in Development and Decay. London: Croom Helm, 1976.

Hutt, Allen. British Trade Unionism, A Short History. London: Lawrence and Wishart, 1975.

Iglitzin, Lynne B., and Ruth Ross, eds. Women in the World: A Comparative Study. Santa Barbara, Calif.: Clio, 1976.

Klüber, Franz. Katholische Soziallehre und demokratischer Sozialismus. Bonn: Neue Gesellschaft, 1974.

Knoll, August M. Katholische Kirche und scholastisches Naturrecht: Zur Frage der Freiheit. Wien: Europa, 1962.

Kolakowski, Leszek. Die Hauptströmungen des Marxismus: Entstehung, Entwicklung, Zerfall, 3 vols. Munich: Piper, 1977, 1978, 1979.

Kreisky, Bruno. Die Zeit in der wir leben: Betrachtungen zur internationalen Politik. Vienna: Molden, 1978.

Künzli, Arnold. Tradition und Revolution: Zur Theorie eines nichtmarxistischen Sozialismus. Basel: Schwabe, 1975.

_____. Karl Marx: Eine Psychographie. Vienna: Europa, 1966.

Ladd, Everett Carll, Jr., and Charles D. Hadley. Transformation of the American Party System, Political Coalitions from the New Deal to the 1970's, 2d ed. New York: W. W. Norton, 1978.

Langner, Albrecht, ed. Katholizismus und freiheitlicher Sozialismus in Europa. Cologne: Bachem, 1965.

La Palombara, Joseph, and Myron Econ Weiner, eds. Political Parties and Political Development. Princeton: Princeton University Press, 1966.

Lehmbruch, Gerhard. Proporzdemokratie: Politisches System und politische Kultur in der Schweiz und in Österreich. Tübingen: Mohr, 1967.

Lenin, I. Wladimir. "Der linke Radikalismus, die Kinderkrankheit im Kommunismus." In Werke, vol. 31, East Berlin: Dietz, 1974.

Lenk, Kurt, and Franz Neumann, eds. Theorie und Soziologie der politischen Parteien. Neuwied: Luchterhand, 1968.

Leonhard, Wolfgang. Die dreispaltung des Marxismus: Ursprung und Entwicklung des Sowjetmarxismus, Maoismus und Reform-kommunismus. Düsseldorf: Econ, 1970

Lepszy, Norbert. Regierung, Parteien und Gewerkschaften in den Niederlanden: Entwicklung und Strukturen. Düsseldorf: Droste, 1979.

Leser, Norbert. Die Odyssee des Marxismus: Auf dem Weg zum Sozialismus. Vienna: Molden, 1971.

Levinson, Charles, ed. Industry's Democratic Revolution. London: George Allen and Unwin, 1974.

Lipset, Seymour M., and Stein Rokkan, eds. Party Systems and Voter Alignments: Cross-national Perspectives. New York: Free Press, 1967.

Luza, Radomir. History of the International Socialist Youth Movement. Leyden: A. W. Sijthoff, 1970.

Macpherson, C. B. Democratic Theory, Essays in Retrieval. Oxford: Clarendon, 1973.

März, Eduard. Einführung in die Marxsche Theorie der Wirt-schaftlichen Entwicklung. Vienna: Europa, 1976.

Matzner, Egon. Wohlfahrtsstaat und Wirtschaftskrise: Österreichs Sozialisten suchen einen Ausweg. Reinbek: Rowohlt,
1978.

Mellors, Collin. The British MP: A Socio-Economic Study of
the House of Commons. Westmead, England: Saxon House,
1978.

Menningen, Walter, ed. Ungleichheit und Wohlfahrtsstaat: Der
Alva-Myrdal Report der Schwedischen Sozialdemokraten.
Reinbek: Rowohlt, 1971.

Merkl, Peter H., ed. Western European Party Systems: Trends
and Prospects. New York: Free Press, 1980.

Miliband, Ralph. Marxism and Politics. Oxford: Oxford University Press, 1977.

_____. Parlamentary Socialism: A Study in the Politics of Labour,
2d ed. London: Merlin Press, 1973.

Miller, Susanne. Die SPD vor und nach Godesberg. Bonn:
Neue Gesellschaft, 1974.

Mills, C. Wright. The Marxists. New York: Delta, 1963.

_____. White Collar: The American Middle Classes. London,
New York: Oxford University Press, 1951.

Nenning, Günther. Realisten oder Verräter? Die Zukunft der
Sozialdemokratie. Munich: Bertelsmann, 1976.

Nugent, Neill, and Roger King, eds. The British Right: Conservative and Right Wing Politics in Britain. Westmead,
England: Saxon House, 1977.

Oberndörfer, Dieter, Hans Rühle, and Hans Joachim Veen, eds.
Sozialistische und Kommunistische Parteien in Westeuropa,
2 vols. Opladen, Westdeutscher, 1978, 1979.

Papcke, Sven. Der Revisionismusstreit und die politische
Theorie der Reform: Fragen und Vergleiche. Stuttgart:
Kohlhammer, 1979.

Paterson, William E., and H. Thomas Alastair, eds. Social Democratic Parties in Western Europe. London: Croom Helm, 1977.

Pelinka, Anton. Gewerkschaften im Parteienstaat: Ein Vergleich zwischen dem Deutschen und dem Österreichischen Gewerkschaftsbund. West Berlin: Duncker and Humblot, 1980.

Potthoff, Heinrich. Die Sozialdemokratie von den Anfängen bis 1945. Bonn: Neue Gesellschaft, 1974.

Raddatz, Fritz J. Karl Marx: Der Mensch und seine Lehre. Hamburg: Hoffmann and Campe, 1975.

Raschke, Joachim. Organisierter Konflikt in Westeuropäischen Parteien: Vergleichende Analyse Parteiinterner Oppositionsgruppen. Opladen: Westdeutscher, 1977.

Raschke, Joachim, ed. Die politischen Parteien in Westeuropa: Geschichte, Programm, Praxis. Ein Handbuch. Reinbek: Rowohlt, 1978.

Reding, Marcel. Der politische Atheismus, 2d ed. Graz: Styria, 1958.

Reilly, Thomas A., and Michael W. Sigall, eds. New Patterns in American Politics. New York: Praeger, 1975.

Revel, Jean-Francois. La tention totalitaire. Paris: Ed. Robert Laffont, 1976.

Roberts, Benjamin, ed. Towards Industrial Democracy: Europe, Japan and the United States. Montclair: Allanheld, Osmun, 1979.

Rose, Richard, ed. Electoral Participation: A Comparative Analysis. Beverly Hills: SAGE, 1980.

____. Electoral Behavior: A Comparative Handbook. New York: Free Press, 1974.

Russell, Bertrand. German Social Democracy. London: George Allen and Unwin, 1965.

Sanford, John. The Mass Media of the German-Speaking Countries. London: Wolff, 1976.

Sartori, Giovanni. Parties and Party Systems: A Framework for Analysis. Cambridge: At the University Press, 1976.

Schaff, Adam. Marxismus und das menschliche Individuum. Vienna: Europa, 1965.

Schleth, Uwe. Parteifinanzen: Eine Studie über Kosten und finanzierung der Parteitätigkeit, zu deren politischer Problematik und zu den möglichkeiten einer Reform. Meisenheim: Anton Hain, 1973.

Schwan, Alexander, and Gesine Schwan. Sozialdemokratie und Marxismus: Zum Spannungsverhaltnis vom Godesberger Programm und Marxistischer Theorie. Hamburg: Hoffmann and Campe, 1974.

Schwan, Gesine. Die Gesellschaftskritik von Karl Marx: Politökonomische und Philosophische voraussetzungen. Stuttgart: Kohlhammer, 1974.

Shell, Kurt L. The Transformation of Austrian Socialism. New York: State University Press, 1955.

Stammen, Theo, ed. Parteien in Europa: Nationale Parteiensysteme, Transnationale Parteienbeziehungen, Konturen eines Europäischen Parteiensystems, 2d ed. Munich: Beck, 1978.

Steininger, Rudolf. Polarisierung und Integration: Eine vergleichende Untersuchung der strukturellen Versäulung der Gesellschaft in den Niederlanden und in Österreich. Meisenheim: Anton Hain, 1975.

Tannahill, R. Neal. The Communist Parties of Western Europe: A Comparative Study. Westport, Conn.: Greenwood Press, 1978.

Vilmar, Fritz, ed. Industrielle Demokratie in Westeuropa: Menschenwürde im Betrieb II. Reinbek: Rowohlt, 1975.

von Beyme, Klaus. Parteien in westlichen demokratien. Munich: Piper, 1982.

_____. Gewerkschaften und Arbeitsbeziehungen in Kapitalistischen Ländern. München: Piper, 1977.

_____. Interessengruppen in der Demokratie. München: Piper, 1969

Wohlgenannt, Rudolf. Der demokratische Sozialismus: Sein Selbstverständnis und sein Verhältnis zum Marxismus. Vienna: Forum, 1978.

Name Index

About the Author

ANTON PELINKA, born 1941 in Vienna, received a Doctor of Law degree in 1964 from Vienna University and then studied political science at the Institute for Advanced Studies in Vienna. After two years working as the political editor for the Viennese weekly paper Die Furche, he became a research assistant at the Institute for Advanced Studies, followed by an assistantship at Salzburg University.

From 1973 to 1975 he was a professor of political science at Essen University in West Germany and Pedagogical College, Berlin (West). He became a professor at Innsbruck University in 1975, where he is presently the chairman of the Department of Political Science. He was a visiting professor at Nehru University in New Delhi in 1977 and at the University of New Orleans in 1981.

In several books, Anton Pelinka published his research outcomes concerning the Austrian political system, democratic theory, and European political parties and labor movements. These books were published in Austria and in West Germany. This is his first book published in the United States.